Effective Learning in Education

ABOUT THE AUTHOR

PANNEER SELVAM is born in Salem - Valappady of Tamil Nadu. He started his career as school teacher in New Delhi in the year 1991. He joins as lecturer in DIET, perundurai of Erode in 2000. Bharathiyar University were gave the Philosophy in Doctorates in Language and Education. He is the seventh diploma holder from National University of Educational Planning and Administration (NUEPA), New Delhi in 2002. In 2005, the Tamil Nadu government was given the 'Excellence Award' for his unrivalled teaching activities and some organization also. He has published more than hundreds of Research Papers and books in the field of Education. At present he is working in the department of Education, Bharathidasan University, Tamil Nadu.

ABOUT THE BOOK

Student's life throughout high school and college is filled thinking about, trying to date, failing to date and being "dumped" the mating game is filled with stress, but it also involves distress, and is among the greatest causes of stress on students. The school environment itself can be a cause of stress on students. Students moving into secondary education find it challenging to constantly move around to classes. Theses matriculating to tertiary education are challenged with leaving home and establishing a new life in a new setting. A student's ambition can be fulfilled only when the mental imagery of him / her gets satisfied. Especially for the students in higher secondary school level, their progress in education marks for choosing their future studies.

❐

Effective Learning in Education

Dr. S.K. Panneer Selvam
Assistant Professor, Department of Education
Bharathidasan University, T.N.,India

AMIGA PRESS INC.

AMIGA PRESS INC.
H.O:- 28-A, Indra Park, St.No-9
Near-Chander Nagar, Krishna Nagar
Delhi: - 110051 (India)
Tel: - 011-22504028, +91-98736-57000
Email: - amigapress@gmail.com
info@amigapress.co.in
amigaeditorial@gmail.com
amigapub@gmail.com

Website: - www.amigapress.co.in

This edition is published by Amiga Press Inc.

ISBN: 978-93-84533-69-4

First Published 2020

Printed and bound in India by Replika Press Pvt. Ltd.

Contents

1

The Problem and its Perspectives

"The mind of man reaches out to grasp the universe" is a poetic statement which is not in the language of science. Man's intellectual processes do try to "reach out to grasp" in the sense that "to grasp" means to make contact with, to hold, and to manipulate. Man is better able to grasp his environment in a literal sense. The Unique skill of man is matched with another unique skill is the ability to talk.

The first qualities of the mind that have to be developed are those which can be grouped under observation. A general perception of an object is we're all usually carried from a cursory half – attentive glance. A closer attention fixes its places, form, nature as distinct from its surrounding full concentration of the faculty of observation gives us all the knowledge that the three chief senses can gather about the object, on if man touch or taste.

IMAGE

Generally, image means a representation, or likeness of a person or object especially in sculpture or in painting. For example, the statue, effigy, the sculptured figure, portrait, picture, curving and the like may be called as image. Image may also mean a visually formed reproduction of an object such as one formed in a mirror. Image also refers to a person or a thing that resembles closely another. It is exactly a copy of the other object or person. Psychologically, image means a mental representation of an object, an idea or a picture produced by a person from his past experience in his imagination. It is the personality characteristics presented to others by a person. The visual meaning of image is the pattern of light that is focused into the retina or the eye. The psychological meaning of an image also is referred to the mental experience of something a person or an object or idea that is not present immediately to the senses, often appearing in the memory as memory image. It is the mental picture or association of ideas elicited from some literary works.

IMAGES AND THINKING

People vary remarkably in how much they use image in their thinking. A few report that they almost never use mental pictures, so they must be doing their thinking with words, or verbally; others report that most of their thinking is done in image form.

When one uses images to think, they are not usually complete "pictures in the head." They are usually incomplete. Consider the imagery you use, if you use it at all, in solving the following problems (Huttenlocher, 1973)

CONCEPT AND MEANING OF MENTAL IMAGERY

The study of mental imagery is a difficult task since it involves thinking of thought process. Man is not only a social animal or doing animal, but also a thinking animal. Among all the functions, thinking alone greatly differentiates man from other animals. The process of thinking is a very broad process which includes imagination, creation and problem solving. All these are mental functions. It is impossible to bring out any clear cut distinction among all these. It is often said that sensations are the gateways of knowledge. But sensations themselves do not become knowledge.

Sensation, perception and learning function together in a dynamic way for evolving the thought process. This takes place only in humans, because it needs the development of complex nervous system and man alone has it. The thought process appears in the form of mental images. The seeing of an object in the outside world forms the images of the object in the mind. And when a name in the form of a word is associated with the object the very mention of the word makes an image of the object in the mind. Thus the ideas relating to the objects or events may appear in the form of images. All the mental images are the reproduction of elements of the past sensation, perception, learning and experiences.

In sensation, perception and learning the human memory plays an active role. They are all stored in the memory by way of impressions. These impressions are not always active. Memory images are the past learned or experienced materials, may come into play in the form of mental activity.

The concepts like the images, imagery, mental images, memory images, after images, eidetic imagery, and associated imagery and so on. But all these are in one way the processes of thinking.

DEFINITION OF MENTAL IMAGERY

Mental imagery has been defined in recent research as a promising strategy for increasing comprehension of discourse (Kulhauy & Swenson, 1975; Lesgold, McCormick & Golinkoff, 1975; Levin, 1973; Steingart &Glock, 1979).Since mental imagery appears to be associated with efficient learning and remembering, it may provide a critical link in explaining the transition from a novice to sophisticated comprehended (Pressley, 1976, 1977).

It is generally agreed that mental imagery has a complex relationship to cognition and language (Hebb, 1966; Piaget &Inhelder, 1971).

The positive effects of induced mental imagery have been carefully documented for paired associate learning (Paivio & Yuille, 1967; Wolff & Levin, 1972; Pressley, 1976)and for listening comprehension(Shimron, 1975; Guttman; Levin& Pressley, 1977).

While recent research has suggested that induced mental imagery facilitates reading comprehension(Pressley, 1976; Steingart & Glock, 1979; Linden & Wittrock,1981) the value of using imagery as a strategy for enhancing reading comprehension has yet to be thoroughly explored (Tierney& Cunningham, in press).

One cause for caution, however, with respect to interpreting the results of the research on mental imagery is that increases in learning from written text are slight while the results of learning from orally presented text have been more substantial .It appears that mental imagery has merit as a strategy for increasing listening comprehension but the value of induced mental. Imagery as a strategy for increasing reading comprehension needs further investigation (Tierney & Cunningham, 1980).

The research to date on induced mental imagery does not provide a direct comparison of the effects of induced mental imagery upon listening and reading comprehension.

PROCESS OF MENTAL IMAGERY

Imagery is generally stated as imageries in plural form in literary works for symbolic representations. Imagery means images in groups. When students wanted they state image collectively it by the concept imagery. Therefore a group of collective images is called imagery. Imageries are the materials involved in the general processes of imagination. Imagery is the distinctive type of men images formed by a particular individual. Psychologically, imagery also refers the mental experience of something that is not immediately present to sense.

The objects of past sensory experiences exist in the memory. Series mental images may be also called as imagery. Therefore there are have various kind of mental images through our sensory experiences such as visual images, auditory images, olfactory images, gustatory images, tactual images, kinaesthesia images and as on.

Generally, painters and artists have more dominant visual images, while the musicians have more dominant auditory images. In blind man the auditory and tactual images are more dominant over other images.

TYPES OF MENTAL IMAGERY

Mental Images

The sensory experiences are the primary causes of the formation of mental images. They move and act only through functions of our senses and their every sense is registering some experiences, whether their like them or not, in their everyday life. Thus every sensory experience from into mental picture and when necessity arises, through some cue or stimulus, it becomes a mental image, drawn from our memory. They are forming images of persons, objects, places, events and experiences. Therefore they may state that a mental image is personal experience of a person about a person, an object or an event that he has formed. These mental images may be referring to visual, auditory, olfactory, gustatory sensation or the sensation of touch. Apart from what the students have already experienced about many things, they are also experiencing everyday many new things.

Visual Images

Among the sensory experiences the visual sensation and experience has a distinctive quality. They see with our eyes every object in front of us. But they cannot give detailed description of all those objects they have seen. Because every object does not possess the sticking characteristics in such a way as to attract our attention and form the image of it. The sensation is get through our eyes is called the vision

Vision means the act of perceiving with our eyes. It may also mean the power of seeing. Through the concept vision is mainly referred here for the sensation of seeing or sight, it has also other meaning. They may say that, he is a man of vision, which means he can fore see things. Vision generally refers to the vivid mental image, vivid picture of what has been seen. It is also used to state a person or object of extraordinary beauty. The concept vision has also philosophical and religious meanings. Thus visual image they may have about many things, a person, place, an event or an object.

Generally human beings are fascinated by the objects or person of extraordinarily beautiful. It is not only referring to beautiful human beings, but also to man's creations like, the paintings of very sensuous and erotic types, the sophisticated sculptures, beautifully designed buildings, architecturally designed and built dams and bridges, machines, cars, planes, ships, arches, printed pictures, books – all these once seen get strong impression in our memory and when they wanted to speak about any of these things they get the mental picture or image of it. All these may appear in their image as they have seen them many days ago.

It is also happening in their life experience to combine the vision to visual sensation and auditory sensation and they may get the image of both visual and auditory. This is what happening in these days in the case of motion pictures and television transmissions. The physical appearance of the actors with the combination of sweet songs in some scenes may cause both the visual images and the auditory images. Even after many years when they hear the song at once the physical images of the artist appear in our mental picture.

Auditory Image

The ear is the sensory apparatus of the auditory images. They might have attended a good musical performance played by a famous songsters or might have seen a beautiful picture drawn by a renowned painter, or a status carved out by a reputed sculptor, or a scène from a famous play or enjoyed a delicious dinner prepared by a skilful cook. All these experiences sometimes make them to think of them or there might have been an occasion for them to narrate it, for which them are making a mental picture of the event and you enjoy it. Actually this is the past experience about the event. Though the object or the event is not present in front of them, they make it to appear before their mental eyes and describe it in detail. Similarly in the case of the musical performance vocal or instrumental performed by a noted musician or a violinist, witnessed by them often make them to have the mental image of the sweet notes ringing in man's ears and enjoy it while describing to others.

Gustatory Images

The tongue is the specialized apparatus of realizing the taste sensation. The mental image of gustatory sensations may make them to go back to our past experience to the days when they ate a dinner with several delicious dishes. The taste of the food often makes to think of it and have the mental image of the incidence. They may have also the images of the taste they disliked. Sometimes they might have discussed with their friends the specific dishes they enjoyed in their hostel day dinner, in a marriage dinner, in a birthday dinner, or some marriage anniversary dinner and so on. In all these, they were able to bright the image of the food from their memory and discuss it. Therefore the sensation of taste once we relished and enjoyed is not lost and we were able to make the image of it mentally.

Olfactory Image

In the experience of enjoying the pleasant sensations by making mental images of them, the olfactory sensation is not falling behind all other sensory images. The nose, particularly the part olfactory epithelium, the smell sensory area is often associated with taste. All the food dishes they eat are tasted with smell. Everything smells and then tasted. Smell and taste are called chemical senses. The fragrant smells of the flowers, the ethereal smells of the fruits, the smells of the delicious dishes prepared by a good cook, the smell or chicken roast or the fish roast, or the smell of the turkey biryani and the smells or fresh food can make you to salivate in your mouth. These smells make good mental images of the scenes.

The garden of the east is noted for its smells. The smells of scents and perfumes of the Arabs were spoken of in the long past. Shakespeare (1566 – 1616) to the Great English dramatic poet, made reference to the perfumes of the Arabia in his play Macbeth. Lady Macbeth had developed the abnormal symptom of fixation and Shakespeare made Lady Macbeth to speak of her abnormalities. She states in one place: "even all the perfumes of Arabs could not change the smell of my hand". Thus Shakespeare had the images of the images of the smells of the perfumes manufactured by the Arabs.

They have the image of not only of the pleasant smells, but also of the unpleasant smells, the sinking's of the garbage in the roads of some cities often make us to have the images of them.

Tactual Images

The touch sensory images are as effective as any other images in their life experience. They touch every object and examine before they purchase at the shopping centers. Why do you want to touch any object before you buy? It is because; only by touching they can tell whether the material is soft or hard, smooth or rough. They also test the texture of the shirting or suiting cloth only by touching. The touch sensation is felt by our skin. Your palm is very sensitive for touches and touching by your palm any abject you can say what sort or surface it has, rough or smooth and so on. The human skin is capable of realizing four sensations such as cold, warmth, pleasure and pain. The sense organs associated with the sensation of touch are called touch spots. These spots are lying below the outer surface of the skin. Some very smooth objects give us pleasant touch sensation and they may often have the image of this touch. A deep pin prick causes painful feeling and at once they jerk back. Sometimes when they go for a medical checkup, one important test is the blood test and blood is taken by fatly pricking one of the finger tips with a sharp needle which causes painful feeling. Therefore whenever they hear about the blood test this incidence from a mental image. Young men are very much inspired by the touch of young women and they often have image of such touches. Hence they have the image of the pleasant and painful touches of their personal life experiences.

Organic Images

Every sensory experience is capable of arousing the mental image if it had strong impression. The organic sensation is felt in their internal organs. The sensations of hunger and thirst are called organic sensations. The sensations of hunger are felt by you when the stomach muscles are contracted. When there is water deficiency in your body you feel dryness in throat and mouth and you feel thirsty. Persons who were without food for several days often have the images of food and food materials. The Caravans pass through desert areas for many days become shorts of water and they often get the image of water springs. It is their feeling thirst for long time makes them to have the images of water. It is their feeling thirst for long time makes them to have the images of water. The European empire builders when they were on long-anxieties. Columbus (1451-1506), an Italian by birth later on became a navigator and an explorer of Spain, who discovered the new world (America) in 1492, had many times the images of the new lands out of fear and anxiety.

The idea, they can evolve from the above discussions is that the formation of image is possible only with keen sensitivity of our sensory instruments to objects, persons, places and events. All of you do not have the same type of vivid visual auditory and other sensory experiences all the times. But everyone will have the vivid sensory experience in some areas at some occasions which might occur even without your will or intention and you might utilize such vivid experience for the formation of images and the same may be used in our symbol thinking. Authors like Moskowitz and Orgel (1969) have started that the symbols are the ideas and symbolic processes are referred to ideational processes and ideas are equal to image.

Memory Images

Text book authors in psychology of the earlier period had been introducing two topics definitely in their books, namely learning and memory. But modern authors write the same topics as learning and remembering. The reason might have been that there is no theory evolved which can be universally acceptable to account for all the phenomena of memory. Therefore memory is dealt with as a process of remembering what have been learned previously. Memory involves learning, retention and remembering.

According to Garrett (1975) memory is classified under four headings such as fixation, retention, recall and recognition.

According to Woodworth (1952) states that memory consists of learning, retaining and remembering what has previously been learned. What Garrett referred as fixation is the efforts taken by the individual for memorizing or getting the impression, which may also state as learning or retention. Retention is the maintenance of the impression or the fixed matter for a period of time. Recall and recognition involve the revival or bringing back to use or re-establishing the learned material on stimulation. All the four components functions together and none of them are independent of the other.

But according to Woodworth retention is not an active process, whereas remembering is an active process and remembering involves recall and recognition. But both the processes, retention and remembering are included under the general heading of memory.

DEVELOPING QUANTITATIVE MENTAL IMAGERY

Moving beyond physical interactions with materials is a significant mathematical step for students that are often difficult to take. Persistent tally-mark use, for example, among older children is a testament to this challenge. For many students, shifting away from tangible tools begins a precarious journey; teachers should support it with thoughtfully tailored instruction. Indeed, this journey begins with helping students "see" math with their "mind's eye" via the construction of quantitative mental imagery. Adapting curriculum materials to support the development of quantitative mental imagery can be as simple as adding a cover to an existing task. For example, if the task involves children adding sections of train cars to determine the entire length of a train, one section might be inside a small tunnel obscuring two or three of the cars. With tasks involving pictorial representations of addition tasks, the picture of the smaller addend could be covered with a sticky note, preventing students from readily counting each perceptual item in the task. However, if needed, the covers can easily be removed to support the development of the quantitative mental image. Given the aim for children to construct an increasingly abstract understanding of mathematics, robust support for mental imagery and re-presentation is of considerable importance. Even a brief series of tasks can afford teachers diagnostic power to design tailored and effective instruction that helps a child transition from materials to mind's eye.

MENTAL IMAGERY AND CURRICULUM

Contemporary trends in education reflect a shift from traditional teacher-cantered approaches to more student-cantered approaches to learning. Empowering students in their own learning is facilitated by teaching them effective meaning-making strategies that support active participation in their own learning. Making this happen requires using "double-duty" instructional strategies that are effective instructional tools for teachers and effective learning tools for students when they work independently without continuous monitoring, feedback, and support. These approaches are popular because they are also effective when used across the curriculum in multiple content areas or disciplines (e.g., in both reading and mathematics instruction as well as in science and social studies). Mental imagery is an effective double duty instructional strategy. In this article, the authors describe a specific mental imagery strategy, the Sensory Activation Model (SAM), developed to assist students in constructing their own images as problem-solving tools. The SAM strategy has been demonstrated to aid students in the construction of self-generated images that facilitate both the reading and writing processes.

Using Mental Imagery to Enhance Children's Motor Performance

Students' motor performance can be enhanced through the use of mental imagery. This article presents nine ways that physical education teachers and coaches can use mental imagery to accomplish various outcomes. These include imagery for: learning, performing, focusing, self-confidence, motivation, arousal, changing negatives into positives, relaxation; and healing.

Classroom Mental Imagery Activity

Describes an activity in which students engage in a size comparison task that replicates the symbolic distance effect: when comparing two imagined objects it takes longer to determine which one is larger if the objects have a small size difference. States that the activity can be used to introduce imagery research.

Mental Imagery in the Teaching Process

Few would argue that students struggle with understanding and representing functions. There are many theories on why the abstraction of mathematical processes poses such cognitive difficulty, but so far functional programming is most often taught in a manner that discourages the use of visual intuition. The paper, by contrast, describes a curriculum for students ages 9 to 15 that addresses the concept of higher-order functions by means of multi-modal imagery building. It discusses the mathematical importance of higher-order functions, outlines the motivation behind the curriculum, and offers a case study of a fifth-grade girl learning functional arguments via computer

Mental Imagery in Multimodal Career Education

Mental imagery, a factor in learning and fantasy, can be used in multimodal career education programs to aid students in speculation about their futures. This multimodal approach addresses areas of human functioning such as behavior, affect, sensation, imagery, cognition, interpersonal relations, and physiology.

CREATIVITY

Creativity as the unique characteristic of the human mind may be defined as the capacity of an individual to create or produce an entirely new or novel idea or object by the rearrangement or reshaping of what is already known. It is both innate as well as acquired and a process as well as a product. It is also characterized by qualities like universality, adventurousness and open-mindedness, a craving for change and novelty, ego involvement and divergent thinking. It does not necessarily have positive correlation with school mental imagery and academic stress.

MENTAL IMAGERY VERBAL PROCESSES

A Developmental Study

A battery of nine tests, including verbal and imagines measures were administered to 200 first- through fifth-grade children. Results revealed that verbal processes and mental imagery developed in a curvilinear manner with parallel rates of change.

Using Mental Imagery and Summarization to Achieve Independence in Comprehension

Recommends teaching both mental imagery (an unobtrusive, natural text processing strategy) and summarizing (an efficient text reorganization strategy) to students who do not spontaneously use them.

Using Mental Imagery to Enhance Gifted Elementary Students' Creative Writing

Examines the effects of mental imagery instruction on 37 gifted fourth and fifth grade students' creative writing and development of imagery vividness. Finds that treatment subjects significantly outperformed control subjects on originality and use of sensory descriptions but not on writing length.

SELF-ATTITUDE ENHANCEMENT THROUGH POSITIVE MENTAL IMAGERY

Enhanced self-attitudes following a psychotherapeutic encounter almost always serve as an indicator of therapy success. In an attempt to enhance self-attitudes through the use of positive mental imagery, undergraduate students (N=72), divided into 4 groups, participated in 4 experimental sessions. The experimental groups imagined themselves exhibiting 10 different desirable personality characteristics (positive imagery) identified as being either common or uncommon self-attributes. The control groups imagined themselves in 10 different outdoor scenes (neutral imagery). To examine the effects of relaxation training on vividness of imagery, two of the groups learned relaxation techniques. All groups participated in three imagery sessions either with or without relaxation training. In the fourth session, which they believed was part of another experiment, the students completed the Tennessee Self-Concept Scale, the Rosenberg Self-Esteem Scale, and a revised Fishbein and Ajzen-type scale of self-attitude, containing the 10 personality characteristics used in the positive imagery condition. Statistical analyses showed that positive imagery significantly affected self-attitude in a positive direction on the Fishbein and Ajzen-type scale but not on the other measures. Enhanced self-attitude resulted primarily from an increase in the affective evaluation of the 10 uncommon personality characteristics.

THE EFFECT OF MENTAL IMAGERY

Undergraduate students who were given specific instructions to form mental images while reading a text passage containing spatial information scored significantly higher than the control group on a drawing post-test. Significant correlations also resulted between the test scores and both reading time and use of imagery. The use of imagery instructions seems to influence the quality of the mental representation and therefore the ability to construct more accurate drawings of the information described in text. Drawing an object from memory is a task that requires the generation of an image in the working memory and reflects the quality of the mental representation. Thus, the use of imagery instructions can be a valuable strategy for learning when the information contains important spatial information.

IMAGERY IMPROVES THE STUDENTS PERFORMANCE

Mental Imagery of the students can be improved in the following ways:

1. The students should be motivated to look for success in their Performance.
2. To acquire the perfection of skills and also to maintain their entry level.

3. The mental ability of his students should be helped to refocus and be calm and relaxed.
4. The mental imagery of the students can be controlled using all their sense organs.
5. The students could also be encouraged to practice and interpret their learning skills appropriately

CONCEPT AND MEANING OF STRESS

Stress is a general term applied to various mental and physiological experienced by people feel in their lives. Stress can mean different things to different people. For some is can theories to take over their lives while for others, once they are aware of its causes and effects, stress can add excitement and challenge to their lives.

Stress can be positive when it motivates us to get things done which are important to his / her. However, it can be negative when we constantly feel pressurized or transmatized by too many demands. Everyone has demand placed on them. They come from their work or being unemployed, from relationships, deadlines, financial problems and illness Humans have to deal with major changes like moving home, changing jobs, getting married or coping with the death of a loved one the way one cope with these demands will depends on the way they think, their personality and their previous life experiences.

" Stress" is a term people often use to describe a feeling of pressure, strain or tension, people often say that they are " under stress" or feel " stressed out" when they are dealing with challenging situations or events.

DEFINITIONS OF STRESS

Stress may be defined as "a state of psychological and / or physiological imbalance resulting from the disparity between situational demand and the individual's ability and / or motivation to meet those demands.

Dr. Hans Selye observes that one of the leading authorities on the concept of stress, described stress as "the rate of all wear and tear caused by life"

Stress can be positive or negative stress can be positive when the situation offers an opportunity for a person to gain something it acts as a motivator for peak performance

Stress can be negative when a person faces social, physical, organizational and emotional problems stress is the body's reaction to a change that requires a physical, mental or emotional adjustments or response.

Stress is often defined as a mismatch between the demands placed on someone and the way she / he cope with these demands. It can have a positive and negative effect.

"Stress" is a term people often use to describe a feeling of pressure, strain or tension. People often say that they are "under stress" or feel "stressed out" when they are dealing with challenging situations or events.

CAUSES FOR STRESS

Stress can come from any situation or thought that makes one feel frustrated, angry, nervous or anxious.

Stress is caused by an existing stress – causing factor or "stressor".

Dealing with a serious illness or caring for someone who is ill can cause a great deal of stress.

ACADEMIC STRESSORS

Academic Stress among students have long been researched on, and researchers have identified stressors as too many assignments, competitions with other students, failures and poor relationships with other students (Fair brother & Warn, 2003).

Academic stressors include the student's perception of the extensive knowledge base required and the perception of an inadequate time to develop it (Carvethetal, 1996).

Students report experiencing academic stress at predictable times each semester with the greatest sources of academic stress resulting from taking and studying from exams, grade competition, and the large amount of contents to master in a small amount of time (Abouserie 1994).

When stress is perceived negatively or becomes excessive, students experience physical and psychological impairment. Methods to reduce stress by students often include effective time management, social support, positive reappraisal and engagement in leisure pursuits (Murphy & Archer, 1996).

The pressure to perform well in the examination or test and time allocated makes academic environment very stressful (Erkutlu & Chafra 2006).

Knowing the causes of students stress will make the educational administrator know how to monitor and control the stress factors that are responsible for the students stress? Often, graduate students perceive that faculty exert great power over their lives and feel that they live in a state of substantial powerlessness (Altbach 1970).

Stressors affecting students can be categorized as academic, financial, time or health related, and self – imposed (Goodman, 1993).

Academic stressors include the student's perception of the extensive knowledge base required and the perception of an inadequate time to develop it (Carvethetal, 1996).

Students reports experiencing academic stress at predictable times each semester with the greatest sources of academic stress resulting from taking and studying for exams, grade competition and the large amount of content to master in a small amount of time (Abouserie, 1994).

The academic stress was measured through its four components namely frustration, conflict, pressure and anxiety.

About frustration, the results show that boys are comparatively more frustrated than girls, while about academic conflicts, the results shows the boys and girls both experienced mental conflicts equally in their academic situation.

About academic pressure the results shows that girl's students perceived more pressure than boys.

About the anxiety the results shows girls were found comparatively more anxious than there boys in their academic situation.

CAUSES OF STRESS ON STUDENTS

Causes of stress on students include both positive and negatives stress, but the focus here is on the causes of negative stress on students. Alphabetically first among the causes of stress on students in academic pressure, simply tacking more difficult assignments can demand stress management techniques.

Student's life throughout high school and college is filled thinking about, trying to date, failing to date and being "dumped" the mating game is filled with stress, but it also involves distress, and is among the greatest causes of stress on students. The school environment itself can be a cause of stress on students. Students moving into secondary education find it challenging to constantly move around to classes. Theses matriculating to tertiary education are challenged with leaving home and establishing a new life in a new setting. Both can use cause stress on students.

Pressure on high school students to engage in extracurricular activities such as choirs, clubs, sports band or volunteer work. The presence of these on a student's application can go for towards acceptance. Once in college, extracurricular activities still cause stress on students, since their presence on a job application is also an asset. Like dating, peer relationships can provide ensures or stress as peer apply pressure in regards to dress, behaviour, choice of friends or music, and many other areas of life, that pressure can becomes a huge cause of stress on students.

High school workloads and later college workloads are heavy for many students. For secondary students planning on tertiary studies, high school grades are important. So is the number of subjects as results students may overload their schedules in college, where a financial investment has been students may overwork to reach their goals and benefit from the money spent workloads at either level are causes of stress on students.

A lack of time management also cause stress on students, whether secondary or tertiary. Balancing academics, dating, peer activities and home life can be difficult loss in a part time job and the challenge increase. Finally, students at either level experiences stress from parental pressure. Parents want their children to succeed in school. They want to see good grades, but they also want to see success in life's other arcas in their attempts to guide their children; parents can become one of the major causes of stress on students.

Stress Related to Academics

Increasing amounts of schoolwork, Assignment deadliness, Quizzes and exams, Class presentations (Public Speaking), Honours and IB classes, High – stakes tests, Getting into college, Selecting a career path, Balancing school with sports, hobbies and social life, Expectations of parents and teachers, Competing with siblings and Fear of failure

Information Age

Academic stress is on the rise party because the information age now provides students with a vast amount of information at their fingertips and because students are expected to synthesize such information at a more accelerated rate than when their parents attended school.

Stress Related to Extracurricular

Sports, Theatre, Clubs, Leadership Positions

Stress Related to Health

Weight, Physical appearance, Self esteem, Diseases / Disabilities, Maturity, Puberty

TYPES OF STRESS

Acute Stress

Acute stress is usually for short time and may be due to work pressure, meeting deadliness pressure or minor accident, over exertion, increase physical activity, searching something the misplaced one or similar things.

Acute Stress Symptoms

The acute stress symptoms are headaches, back pain, stomach problems, rapid heartbeat, muscle aches or body pain. Acute stress is common in people who take too many responsibilities and are overloaded or overworked, disorganized, always in a hurry and never in time. These people are generally in positions of importance at their workplace and stressful lifestyle is inherent in them.

Physical Stress

This occurs when the body as a whole starts to suffer as a results of a stress full situation. Symptoms can manifest in a variety of ways and vary in their seriousness. The most common physical symptom is headaches because stress cause people to unconsciously tense their neck, forehead and shoulder muscles. However, long term stress can lead to digestive problems including ulcers, insomnia, fatigue, high blood pressure nervousness and excessive sweating, heart disease, strokes and even hair loss.

Emotional Stress

These response are due to stress affecting the mind and include anxiety, anger, depression, irritability, frustration, over reaction to everyday problems, memory loss and a lack of concentration for any task.

Academic Stress

The pressure from parents, which is predominantly bringing stress on the students. The environment in the house, such as big family with lot of adults and playful children, is another pressure on students to get Academic Stress. Poverty in the family is also another reason for Academic Stress. Broken family, particularly separated father and mother, tells on the teen age children very badly. This tragedy psychologically affects the students and makes them suffer Academic Stress

ACADEMIC STRESS

Stress or tension, has become an integral part of our daily life. A little bit of stress may be unavoidable and good too, for it would never allow us to be complacent in life. But too much of stress may be counterproductive and would in due course impair both our physical and mental health.

And such stress stalks all the age-groups including the children and the youth. Education should be a joyous experience, but if too much pressure is put into it, children find the going a hard nut to crack.

Too much of home work, home work during the long summer vacations and the tedious examination system, all have made both the wards and their parents edgy. There are hundreds of cases of youngsters taking their lives when they fail in the examination.

Failure in an examination is not the end of the life. One can excel in any field if one chooses the right field for which one has the aptitude.

It is the duty of parents, the schools, the colleges, the universities and the educational authorities to make education stress-free. They have to reorient education with the child or the youth as the centre, removing all the obstacles that come in the way of the development of an integrated personality.

To a large extent, a part of the stress can be eased by promoting a harmonious relationship between the parents on one hand the children on the other and also between the wards and the educational institutions. The parents should take an immense interest in what their child learns at the school and should do their best in attending the periodical parent- teacher meetings. All efforts should be made to sustain the trilateral interaction among the three-the student, the teacher and the parents

NEED FOR THE STUDY

A student's ambition can be fulfilled only when the mental imagery of him / her gets satisfied. Especially for the students in higher secondary school level, their progress in education marks for choosing their future studies. Hence the higher secondary school is said to be a crucial stage in the academic life of students. It is said to be a foundation stage for college learning and to establish successful career. Every student should be enlightened with better school imagery to attain interest in the field of education.

Higher secondary school students are mostly adolescents. Adolescents in a highly critical period in the life of all students to choose their own interest in their field of education.

The school imagery is an important trait among the student's especially higher secondary school students. The importance of the study is to focus mainly with the higher secondary school students whether the two variables-Mental Imagery and Academic Stress are inter-related and whether there is a mutual interdependence. The findings may lead to suitable measure to improve the mental imagery to bring about the interest in education of the higher secondary school students and also to lower the academic stress that the higher secondary school students experiment in today's competitive learning environment.

STATEMENT OF PROBLEM

"Mental Imagery and Academic Stress of Higher Secondary School Students"

OPERATIONAL DEFINITION OF KEY TERM

Mental Imagery

By this the investigator means the scores obtained from the Mental Imagery constructed and standardised by Pressley and Levin (2014) administered among the higher secondary school students.

Academic Stress

By this the investigator means the overall score obtained by the higher secondary school students on the academic stress scale by S. Mani (2012).

OBJECTIVES OF THE STUDY

1. To find out the level of mental imagery among higher secondary school students.
2. To find out the level of academic stress among the higher secondary school students.
3. To find out the significant difference in mental imagery along with its dimensions among the higher secondary school students with respect to,
   - Gender
   - Medium of Instruction
   - Type of Management
   - Type of Family
   - Birth Order
4. To find out the significant difference in academic stress among the higher secondary school students with respect to,
   - Gender
   - Medium of Instruction
   - Type of Management
   - Type of Family
   - Birth Order
5. To find out the significant relationship between mental imagery and its dimension and academic stress among the higher secondary school students.
6. To find out the significant correlation between mental imagery and academic stress among the higher secondary school students.

SIGNIFICANCE OF THE STUDY

Imagery is a flow of thoughts one can see, hear, feel, smell, or taste. Throughout this program, one will see these three terms: imagery; guided imagery; and Interactive Guided Imageries. It's important to recognize the differences between the three:

- Imagery is a natural, yet special, way of thinking that involves our senses. Images are thoughts you can see, hear, smell, taste or feel, and include memories, dreams and daydreams, plans and visions, and fantasies. Imagery is a type of thinking that has particularly strong effects on our emotions (imagine the face of someone you love and notice the feelings that come with the image), and our physiology (close your eyes and imagine sucking on a really sour lemon).

- Guided imagery describes a process where you are asked to focus on images selected to help you achieve certain goals. Common applications include relaxation, relieving pain and other physical symptoms, reducing distress from surgery and other medical procedures, increasing creativity, enhancing confidence, stimulating healing responses in the body, and enhancing memory and learning.
- Interactive Guided Imagery is a specific way of using imagery with particular applications in mind/body medicine. It is particularly effective in helping you to discover and improve their relationship to your health, to discover what role their can play in their recovery, and in helping you to use your resources most effectively. In this form of imagery, a trained guide helps to discover and work with your personal imagery about their illness and you're healing, clarify any issues that may be involved, and learn to use their mind to support your own healing.

The imagination, as it is used in imagery, is not sufficiently valued in the Indian culture. The imaginary is equated with the fanciful, the unreal, and the impractical. In school students are taught the three R's while creativity, uniqueness, and interpersonal skills are either barely tolerated or frankly discouraged. As adults, people are usually paid to perform tasks, not to think creatively. The premium is on the practical, the useful, the real, as it should be- but imagination should be recognized as a valuable component of human thought.

Without imagination, humanity would be long extinct. It took imagination-the ability to conceive of new possibilities-to make fire, create weapons, and cultivate crops; to construct buildings, invent cars, airplanes, space shuttles, television, and computers.

Paradoxically, their collective imagination, which has allowed them to overcome so many natural threats, has been instrumental in creating the major survival problems students face on earth today-pollution, exhaustion of natural resources, and the threat of nuclear annihilation. Yet imagination, teamed with will, remains our best hope for overcoming these same problems.

The focus is primarily on simple ways of using imagery for relaxation, stress reduction, and emotional wellness.

Four significant factors were found to contribute to academic stress: peer pressure; parental pressure; importance of school; and fear of failure. Peer pressure was found to vary across all variables. Importance of school and fear of failure were found to vary across ethnicity, sex, and grade. If the aim of many guidance and counseling programs is to reduce academic stress, then different goals are suggested reflecting appropriate levels of ethnicity, sex, and grade. Consideration must also be given to the predominance of academic stressors emanating from non-school sources, such as the family, parents, and peers, rather than school factors such as teachers.

While many students will experience school-related stress, it is the ability to cope with the stress that matters. Some consequences of stress are mild, such as occasionally losing a few hours of sleep or skipping a meal while trying to meet a deadline. Serious negative consequences can also occur, however. Stress lowers immunity. It can cause insomnia, especially when sleep is interrupted, inconsistent, or too short. Some students try to relieve stress with drinking alcohol or taking drugs.

The school is building an effective mental representation. It would be valuable to gather much different mental representation imagery, and to test their effectiveness, the different parameters that play a role in the way students receive them, and the condition under which they can be useful this is the effort we started at a small scale. Our opinion is that the more we are able to build mental representations imagery, the more they are able to think effectively as students or researcher.

The school year can be hard on anyone. Academic stress can build upon self-esteem issues, family, friends and even the individual concerned. When not taken care of, one's performance suffers, morale suffers, and life just suffers. Instead of being on the brink of a constant freak out, grab life by the horns and get to relaxing. It may be easier than one think.

DELIMITATION OF THE STUDY

This investigation has the following delimitation

- The sample is limited to 348 students
- The sample is taken only from Chennai, in Tamil Nadu
- The sample is higher secondary school students only
- The sample are taken only from 1 Government School, 1 Government Aided School, 2 Matriculation School

CONCLUSION

The problem of the present study has been discussed briefly in this chapter, bringing out of the significance of the study. Objectives of the study etc. The terms operationally defined in this study. A review of the related literature available has been scanned to the theoretical perspective in this study to throw light for formulating appropriate hypothesis which could be tested. A detail discussion of the related literature follows in the next chapter.

❐

2

Review of Related Literature

This chapter deals with the ideal suggestion and research work of the previous researchers in the field of Mental Imagery and academic Stress.

PURPOSE OF THE REVIEW OF LITERATURE

Review of related literature, besides allowing the researchers to acquaint himself with current knowledge in the field or area in which he is going to conduct his research, server the following specific purposes.

The review of related literature enables the researchers to defines the limits of his fields, it helps the researcher to delimit and define his problem, the knowledge of related literature, brings the researchers up to date on the work which other have done and thus to state the objectives clearly and concisely.

The review of related literature gives the researcher an understanding of the research methodology which refers to the way and study to be conducted. It helps the researchers to know about the tools and instruments which prove to be useful and promising in the previous study. The advantages of the related literature also help to provide insight in to the statistical methods through which validity of results are to be established.

STUDIES ON MENTAL IMAGERY

Levin and Divine – Hawkins (1974) A study was to investigate the effects of induced mental imagery upon the comprehension of oral versus written discourse for above and below average readers. A secondary purpose was to determine, through a follow-up interview, the students' ability to induce mental imagery. A study investigated the hypothesis that mental imagery facilitates access to prior knowledge and therefore enhances the ability to infer and make text-relevant predictions. The subjects, 29 first grade and 29 third grade students, were randomly assigned to either an experimental group where they were instructed to make pictures in their head to help them remember the story as they read, or a control group where they were told simply to think about what they were reading to help them remember. A short story, which was written at first grade and third grade readability levels, was divided into five sections at points in the story where predictions about forthcoming events could be made and used as stimuli. Immediately following the silent reading of each of the five sections of the story, the subjects responded to a prediction question. The recorded responses were scored for reference to explicit facts, prediction statements, and accuracy of prediction. The results supported the hypothesis that induced mental imagery enhances the ability to infer and make text predictions for third grade students, but not for the younger subjects.

Pressley's (1976) The findings of this study provide support for the conclusion that induced mental imagery facilitates reading comprehension for children of third grade and above and the results of this study, indicate that induced mental imagery does not enhance reading comprehension for beginning readers. That induced mental imagery appears to facilitate listening comprehension for children as young as first grade research further suggests that younger children rely more on imagery in memory retrieval of orally presented information than do older children. The findings may reflect an age/ experience effect with respect to mental imagery under reading conditions. Another, perhaps more obvious explanation, is that proficient readers benefit from induced mental imagery while, for younger, less proficient readers inducing mental imagery adds an additional processing burden (processing mental images and print simultaneously).An inspection of the means for the first graders in the imagery and non-imagery groups suggests, however, that there were no detrimental effects from instructions to induced mental imagery.

Kosslyn's (1976) This study support the hypothesis that induced mental imagery facilitates access to prior knowledge and therefore enhances the ability to infer and make text relevant predictions for third graders. This hypothesis was based on three assumptions: first, that the use of mental imagery facilitates interaction between the reader and the text; second, that the use of mental imagery facilitates access to text relevant prior knowledge; third, that induced mental imagery is more effective than spontaneous imagery.

Pressley (1976) and Olshaysky (1977) The magnitude of the effect of induced mental imagery upon the recall of facts stated in the story and the generation of text relevant predictions for third grade subjects in this study is of particular interest. These findings strongly suggest that reader-text interaction is enhanced by induced mental imagery. Other studies investigating the effects of mental imagery on reading comprehension have generally reported statistical differences of such low magnitude that they are of questionable educational value .Previous research on reading and mental imagery has focused on subject's responses to literal and, to a lesser extent, inferential questions. In this study subjects responded to open-ended prediction questions. While the speculation is tentative, it may be that imagery facilitates language elaboration and that open-ended prediction questions are more sensitive to the effects of induced mental imagery than more focused cued recall questions. In this study the findings for third grade subjects suggest that they were highly sensitive to instructions to induce mental imagery about what they read. While there is evidence to suggest that some children spontaneously image the results of this study support the contention that induced mental imagery is more effective than spontaneous imagery for third graders. Investigated were the role of mental imagery in children's logical reasoning and individual differences in children's use of imagery while reasoning. Fifth grade students assessed as being high imagers (HIS) and low imagers (LIS) completed conditional syllogisms of various kinds and were asked, after each of their responses, whether an image had occurred to them in the course of solving the problem. Results indicated that (1) HIS and LIS groups were differentiated in terms of their imagery reports when the content of the problem was low in imagery value (2) both groups appeared to use imagery for inferences which do not yield either a definite "yes" or "no" conclusion (3) for inferences of intermediate difficulty, LIS appeared to use imagery unsuccessfully, while HIS appeared to use it successfully. This difference does not seem to be due to a general difference in ability, as both groups' performance on a different, difficult memory task was equivalent. It is thought that this difference may stem from the fact that LIS may not have adequate procedures for integrating imagery with abstract verbal processes. A number of other results of general interest are also reported and discussed. Taken together, results provide preliminary evidence that the image ability of material included in problems does not have a facilitative effect for all students.

This project investigates the role of mental imagery in logical reasoning in children, and, more specifically, individual differences in that respect. Previous results in this line of research have indicated that imagery appears to be used by children in deductive inference, at least in some cases, but that imagery is used successfully only when children have a basic understanding of the logic of the problem. Fifth graders, assessed as being High imagers and Low imagers respectively, answered conditional syllogisms of various kinds and were asked, after each of their responses, whether an image occurred to them in the course of solving the problem. Results indicated that (0 the two groups of children were differentiated in terms of their imagery reports when the content of the problem was low in imagery value (as assessed previously in a separate task); when the content of the problem was high in imagery value, the two groups differed to a much lesser. Extent in terms of their imagery reports; (ii) both groups appeared to use imagery. For most difficult inferences, that is, for those 'indeterminate' inferences which don't yield either a definite 'yes" conclusion or a definite 'no' conclusion; for those inferences; however, the(apparent) use of imagery did not improve performance in solving the problem, thus suggesting again that, in order to be effective, imagery must be monitored by logical processes of a deeper kind; however, (iii) for inferences of intermediate difficulty (Modus Tollens), which are known to be partly mastered by children of that age, an interesting difference occurred: Low imagers appeared to use imagery unsuccessfully, while High imagers appeared to use it successfully; this difference does not seem to be due to a general difference An ability between the two groups ,as their performance on a different, difficult memory task was equivalent; it is speculated that this difference may stem from the fact that Low imagers, who don't tend to rely on imagery, may not have adequate procedures for integrating it with abstract verbal processes.

STUDIES ON ACADEMIC STRESS

For any specific research project to occupy a place in the development of a discipline, the researcher must be thoroughly familiar with both previous theory and researches carried out in that field. To assure this familiarity, every research project in the behavioural science has one of its early stages a review of the theoretical and research literature. An attempt has been made in this chapter to present a review or researches available in this particular field of for gaining acquaintance with the present status of the research work done in the area under study with a hope to provide a perspective to ascertain the general trends in the field. It may provide the insight and direction which may help to identify the problem.

Berlyne, (1967) A large body of research indicates that as arousal increases, task performance many rise at first.

Maslach, (1982) Pines & Aronson, (1988) In most jobs involve at least a degree of stress. Yet somehow the persons performing them manage to cope they continue to function despite their daily encounters with various stressors some individuals, though, are not so lucky. Over time, they seem to be worn down by repeated encounters with stress. Such persons are said to be suffering from burnout, and they show several distinctive characteristics.

Hefferin (1982) adds that younger students often develop intimate psychosocial relationships at this time in their lives. Older students, however, also have stressors unique to their age group.

Gaines &Jermier, (1983) Poor opportunities for promotion and the presence of inflexible rules and procedures lead individuals to feel that they are trapped in an unfair system and to develop negative views of their jobs.

Steers, (1984).,Motowidlo, Packard, & Manning, (1986); This relationship may hold true under some conditions, growing evidence suggests that even low or moderate levels of stress can interfere with task performance.

Whitman (1985) Research indicates that an individual's age may have an influence on his or her perceived stress level. Suggests that younger students experience many stressful changes in their lives. These students often leave home for the first time when going away to school. Often, they experience ambivalent feelings resulting from the need for parental/familial support and the drive for independence. Additionally, the academic expectations in college can be an abrupt change from those in high school. The pressure to achieve good grades can result in a battle for self-esteem

Jackson, Schwab, & Schuler, (1986) Job conditions implying that one's efforts are useless, ineffective, or unappreciated seem to contribute to burnout.

Green (1987) states that older students will have to deal with more decisions about career commitment, alterations in family relationships and planning for financial security. They often have more roles that compete for their time and energy

Taylor (1991) Social support may be an important buffer against the adverse effects of chronic stress. Some recent evidence suggests that the effects of stress on our immune system may be less for people who have effective ways of dealing with their stressors than for those who do not. For example, some studies have shown that optimism, regular exercise, and feelings of control over stressful events are associated with reduced suppression of our immune system under stress.

Beck & Srivastava (1991) found that high school students suffer from long hours of study, multiple assignments, lack of free time, lack of timely feedback and lack of faculty response to student needs.

Bell (1991) Lengacher, (1996); Green, (1987); Beck, (1995) found that anxiety and stress could interfere with learning a complex, psychomotor skill. Other studies identify social factors as a major source of stress in high school students

Kiecolt Glaser and Glaser, (1992) The link between stress and personal health, according to medical experts, is very strong indeed . In fact, some authorities estimate that stress plays some role in 50 to 70 percent of all physical illness . To list just a few, stress has been implicated in the occurrence of heart disease, high, blood pressure, hardening of the arteries, ulcers, and even diabetes.

Melamed, Kushnir, &Shiron, (1992) Studies report many symptoms of physical strain, such as frequent headaches, nausea, poor sleep, and changes in eating habits. Burnout may also be associated with risk factors for cardiovascular disease.

Hamill (1995) found that high school students often have difficulty adjusting to the academic environment of secondary education, as well as difficulty adjusting to the environment of a high school. Studies indicate that the practical & lab component of high school is the most stressful.

Mahat, (1996); Kleehamer, Hart &Fogel, (1990); Admi, (1997). Pagana (1988) surveyed 262 high school students and found that personal inadequacy and a fear of making mistakes were constant stressors. He also found that time management problems, when trying to complete home work, added to a student's perception of stress.

Nunnery (1997) states that, older students sometimes believe that they do not fit in. In some cases, these students are more prone to test and computer anxiety.

Sarafino &Ewing, (1999)., Hudd et al., (2000); Misra& McKean, (2000); Peden et al., (2001); Females usually report a higher level of self-imposed stress and report more physiological reactions to stressors than males. Then they states that females have often been socialized to be "good little females" and not to be self-reliant. Females are expected to depend on others and to look to others for approval. Females also tend to be involved in more activities such as taking care of families, working and attempting to achieve academic excellence. Misra& McKean (2000) believe that men may report lower stress levels as they have been socialized to be self-reliant and that a show of emotion is an expression of weakness and not masculine

This study sought to investigate the factors contributing to academic stress within an adolescent student population, and whether these factors vary across ethnicity, sex, and grade. The Academic Pressure Scale for Adolescents was administered to 550 high school students.

This study sought to investigate the factors contributing to academic stress within an adolescent student population, and whether these factors vary across ethnicity, sex and grade. The Academic Pressure Scale for Adolescents was administered to 550 students and four significant factors were found to contribute to academic stress: peer pressure; parental pressure; importance of school; and fear of failure. Peer pressure was found to vary across ethnicity and grade, but not across sex. Parental pressure was found to be consistent across all variables. Importance of school and sear of failure were found to vary across ethnicity, sex and grade. These variations are discussed in relation to ethnic, grade and gender influences.

Hansel, (1985); Siddique & D'Arcy, (1984); Toylor& Murphy, (1985); Yamamoto, Silliman, Pearsons& Davies, (1987) has cited the school as a major contributor to student stress. As a considerable proportion of teenager's life is spent at school in the pursuit of academic endeavors, it is reasonable to assume that a substantial proportion of stressors affecting adolescents may originate in the academic area. Little research has been undertaken, however, which attempts to determine the origins of academic stress within the school system.

The existing literature on stress in adolescence reveals several sources of stress to which adolescents find themselves vulnerable in their ongoing social interactions. Donald, 1973; Ficula, 1983; (Siddique & D'Arcey, 1984; Hansel, 1985; Tolor&Murphy, 1985; Garzarelli, Hoxter& Lester, 1987 Yamamoto et al., 1987The stressors emanating from the family, school and peer groups are of particular importance. It is in these three spheres of life that adolescents spend most of their time and in which most of their stressful events occur. Since the family, school and peer group form the major socializing influences on adolescents, the expectations or demands they make may convert into stressors. Further, adolescents may perceive these expectations as limiting their behaviour or counter to their own predispositions which may increase the impact of such stressors.

DISCUSSION AND CONCLUSION

The results of the comparison of the effects of induced mental imagery under listening and reading conditions are not consistent with the research which suggests that induced mental imagery is more potent for listening than for reading comprehension (Pressley, 1977).The results of the present study suggest that instructions to induce mental imagery maybe equally effective under listening and reading conditions. It should be noted that the study attempted to eliminate and reduce major methodological problems inherent in the existing research which has prohibited direct comparisons of the effects of induced mental imagery for listening and reading comprehension of discourse.

Above average males recalled more higher level propositions than above average females, however, below average females recalled more than below average males under both listening and reading conditions. The same effect was found with respect to lower level propositions under the reading condition. The statistically significant sex and ability interactions found in this study suggest that sex differences may be a promising area for future research.

The results of the interview on use of mental imagery revealed that under the listening condition 17% of the below average subjects reported that they were not able to induce mental imagery while only 3% of the above average readers reported they were unable to do so. Under the reading condition 21% of the below average readers and 6% of the above average readers reported they were unable to induce mental imagery. More below average readers than above average readers report an inability to induce mental imagery. As Tierney and Cunningham (1980) have suggested further research is needed to determine how imagery may be effectively induced since a rather large percentage of below average readers in the study apparently had difficulty imaging.

Finally, the results of the investigation lead to two additional conclusions. First, the results support the findings of Smiley et al.(1977) and Guthrie (1973) which suggest that poor readers suffer from specific comprehension difficulties which do not appear to involve decoding skills. There were large differences between above and below average reader's comprehension performance under both listening and reading conditions. Second, the data are also consistent with the assumption that listening and reading comprehension depend upon the same basic process.

These findings suggest that there are gender specific differences in the perceived antecedents of academic stress, with girls tending to experience more stress than boys. However, the fact that boys and girls did not show significant differences on 27 of the 35items comprising the scale is indicative of the fact that for many areas of the academic arena gender based differences in the perceived antecedents of academic stress do not exist. This may help to explain some of the disagreement in the literature. The interesting question now becomes: what is the cause(s) of the differential performance on those eight items on which boys and girls differed significantly

Further research should assess effective ways of ameliorating the academic stress on our adolescent youth and, based on the findings of this study, particularly from adolescent girls. This can only be achieved by first increasing our understanding of those stressors originating from the academic environment, their effects on the developing adolescent, and other factors besides gender which may play a part in the effects of academic stress including cultural background, age, grade, socioeconomic status, academic aspirations, and academic ability.

As we progress towards the next millennium the negative effects of stress will likely continue to affect the adolescent members of our society. By attempting to focus on those stressors which are peculiar to adolescence and on the responses by adolescents (Zambrana& Silva-Palacios, 1989), researchers should be able to both identify the sources of stress and determine ways to reduce the deleterious effects of stress. Bearing in mind the importance of education, the reduction of academic stress among adolescents through a greater understanding of this complex but costly phenomenon is a particularly worthwhile goal.

CONCLUSION

In this chapter, research results of the past investigators are taken into account and denoted so that it may avoid overlapping of the research topic. Also it mentions the significance of variables, their correlation etc, on which the research is done.

❐

3

Methodology

This chapter gives an overall picture of design of the study, the form of hypotheses to be tested, research tools used for the data collection, reliability and validity of the tools, scoring procedure, pilot study, nature and collection of the sample, a brief description of the procedure adopted for the data collection, and statistical techniques to be employed for the analysis of the data. Hence the present chapter serves as a guide to research, to show how all the major part of the project the objectives, the review of literature, hypotheses and statistical techniques work together to address the central research questions

STATEMENT OF THE PROBLEM

The present study is entitled as *"Mental Imagery and Academic Stress of higher secondary school students"*

HYPOTHESES OF THE PROBLEM

The following hypotheses have been framed by the researcher for the present study.

1. The levels of mental imagery of higher secondary school students are moderate in nature.
2. The level of academic stress of higher secondary school students is moderate in nature.

3. There is no significant difference in the visual dimension of mental imagery among higher secondary school students with respect to
    - Gender
    - Medium of Instruction
    - Type of Management
    - Type of Family
    - Birth Order
4. There is no significant difference in the Auditory dimension of mental imagery among higher secondary school students with respect to
    - Gender
    - Medium of Instruction
    - Type of Management
    - Type of Family
    - Birth Order
5. There is no significant difference in the Gustatory dimension of mental imagery among higher secondary school students with respect to
    - Gender
    - Medium of Instruction
    - Type of Management
    - Type of Family
    - Birth Order
6. There is no significant difference in the Olfactory dimension of mental imagery among higher secondary school students with respect to
    - Gender
    - Medium of Instruction
    - Type of Management
    - Type of Family
    - Birth Order
7. There is no significant difference in the Tactual dimension of mental imagery among higher secondary school students with respect to
    - Gender
    - Medium of Instruction
    - Type of Management
    - Type of Family
    - Birth Order
8. There is no significant difference in the Bodily dimension of mental imagery among higher secondary school students with respect to

- Gender
- Medium of Instruction
- Type of Management
- Type of Family
- Birth Order

9. There is no significant difference of academic stress among higher secondary school students with respect to
    - Gender
    - Medium of Instruction
    - Type of Management
    - Type of Family
    - Birth Order
10. There is no significant correlation between mental imagery and academic stress of higher secondary school students.

METHOD OF THE STUDY

As, the study intends to collect data pertaining to mental imagery and academic stress among higher secondary school students, survey method is employed to describe and interpret what exists at presents. The survey methods gather data from a relatively large number of cases at a particular time. It is not concerned with characteristics of individuals as individuals. It is concerned with the statistics that result when data are abstracted from a number of individual cases.

VARIABLES OF THE STUDY

The present investigation includes the following variables.

1. Independent Variables - Mental Imagery
2. Dependent Variables - Academic Stress
3. Back ground Variables:
    - Gender
    - Medium of Instruction
    - Type of Management
    - Type of Family
    - Birth Order

TOOLS AND TECHNIQUES USED

To test the hypotheses formulated, the following tools have been used in the present study.

1. Personal data sheet developed by the investigator.

2. Mental Imagery developed and standardized by Rajamanickam. M (2014) was adopted.
3. Academic Stress developed and Standardized by Mani. S (2012) adopted.

DESCRIPTION OF THE TOOL

Mental Imagery

Mental Imagery Questionnaire as it is designed to assess the sensory experiences of the individuals. The mental imagery questionnaire consists of six subs – test referring to six areas of sensory experiences. The areas of sensory experiences are (1) visual, (2) auditory, (3) gustatory, (4) Olfactory, (5) tactual, and (6) bodily. Each one is a test.

On the determining the reliability and validity of each test by the method of item discrimination analysis 15 items in each area which were highly reliable were selected. Thus on the whole (15 X 6) 90 items were retained on the basis and high discriminatory power of the statements. The rest of them were dropped. Therefore, the final form of each sensory area has 15 items which constitute a sub – test. All the six areas have uniformly 15 items. In each test, all the 15 items are referring to an event of the experience which everyone might have had in his / her life.

The mental imagery questionnaire is designed and developed on the pattern of liker scaling technique as a six – point scale with six subs – test. Each test is independent and measure only one aspect. Since the weights are given as 5, 4,3,2,1 and 0 for very clear, fairly vivid, just clear, somewhat clear, dim and no image respectively and each item is rated with these weights the highest possible score, if a person rated all the 15 items with the weight of 5 is 75 (15 X 5) and if the person rated all the 15 items with the weight of 0, then the lowest possible score is (15 X 0). But the rating chances for higher ratings are with the weights 5, 4,3 and the chances for the lower ratings are with weight 0,1,2 But generally no person would rate all the item with the weight of 5 and no person would rate all the items with the weight of 0 Therefore the highest point 75 and the lowest point 0 will never take place, unless there were some extraordinary cases of one or two in a big sample.

Administration

The Mental Imagery Questionnaire is used to assess the level of mental imagery of an individual in six possible sensory areas. The six sensations including in this testing are sight, sound, taste, smell, touch and body sensation. This can be used as an individual test and also as a group test. The participant should be seated comfortably in a well illuminated room where there are no visual and auditory distractions.

You have to Assign the Weights of the Responses

Very Clear and vivid image	Score 5
Fairly vivid image	Score 4
Just Clear	Score 3
Somewhat clear	Score 4
Dim Image	Score 1
No Image	Score 0

Scoring

The mental imagery responses are to given in the booklet itself. Against each item of the inventory 6 alternatives are given in the form of cell indicating the intensity of the responses. Assign 5 marks to " very clear and vivid image", 4 marks to " Fairly vivid image", 3 marks to " Just clear", 2 marks to " Somewhat clear", 1 mark to " Dim image", 0 marks to " No image".

TABLE. 3.1: Showing the Range of Scores and the Norms

S. No	Range of Scores	Degree of Mental Imagery	Weight
1	67.6 - 75.0	Very clear and vivid image	5
2	52.6 - 67.5	Fairly vivid image	4
3	37.6 - 52.5	Just clear image	3
4	22.6 - 37.5	Somewhat clear image	2
5	7.6 - 22.5	Dim image	1
6	0 - 7.5	No image	0

DESCRIPTION OF THE TOOL

Academic Stress Inventory

To analyze the higher secondary school boys and girls students academic stress, the Academic stress Inventory developed and standardized by S. Mani (2012) was adapted. The Academic Stress Inventory developed consists of 54 items each one comprising of five alternatives, namely: Always, Often, Frequently, rarely, never. All the 54 items are negatives.

Administration

The tool was administered to those higher secondary school boys and girls students who had been randomly chosen from the higher secondary school students. The following instructions were given.

1. Given below are the statements regarding academic stress

2. Five alternatives are given beside every statement as always, often, frequently, rarely, never.
3. Put a tick mark (√) against the alternatives which is most suitable in your opinion.
4. There is no time limit. However you are requested to complete the task as quickly as possible.

Scoring Procedure

Maximum possible score is 216 and the minimum score is 0. The high score indicates more academic stress and low score indicates low academic stress. 4 marks are allotted to 'always',3 marks are allotted to 'often',2 marks are allotted to 'frequently',1 marks are allotted to 'rarely',0 marks to the response are 'never' .

Pilot Study

A pilot study was conducted among 50 higher secondary school students which were not included for the main study, to establish the reliability and validity of the different research tools used in this study.

RELIABILITY AND VALIDITY OF THE TOOLS

MENTAL IMAGERY

Reliability

The reliability and the validity are the six sub-tests were tested with their reliabilities and validities. The internal consistency procedure was adapted for determining the reliability of the six sub- tests. The item discrimination analysis was used to eliminate the inconsistent items.

Validity

The six sub-tests were validated with content validity since the content validity or the face validity is considered to be exclusively a logical type of validity for any type of instrument. The researcher is fully satisfied with the items of the instrument that each item is referring to only a specific quality. If the investigator is satisfied with this characteristic of the instrument the instrument is supposed to be a valid one and can be used to any population.

ACADEMIC STRESS INVENTORY

Reliability

In order to establish the reliability of the Academic Stress Inventory the odd-even methods of reliability was used. The reliability of academic stress inventory was found to be 0.96. Hence, academic stress inventory was considered to be reliable and suitable for the present study.

Validity

The index of validity which is the square root of reliability. The validity of the Academic Stress Inventory was found to be 0.98 which is more valid and suitable for the present study.

SAMPLE OF THE STUDY

Data was collected from the higher secondary students adopting stratified random sampling method. The total sample size was 348 drawn from four schools, selected for the study belonging to different types of Management: *Government, Government Aided, Private* schools in Tamil Nadu. The details of the schools visited and the number of students tested for investigation are given below.

TABLE. 3.2: Distribution of the Sample
Showing the details of the sample selected from different types of management of schools

Types of Management	Sl. No	Name and place of the school	Male	Female	Total
Government School	1	Dhanalakshmi Government girls & boys higher secondary school, Chennai	55	60	115
Government Aided School	2	Dhanalakshmi Nadar Higher Secondary school, Chennai	60	50	110
Private School	3	St. Thomas Matriculation Higher secondary school, Chennai	37	25	123
	4	Sheba Matriculation Higher Secondary School, Chennai	30	31	
	Total				348

STATISTICAL TECHNIQUES USED

a. Mean

$$\text{Mean } (\overline{x}) = A + \frac{\sum fd}{\sum f} \times i$$

Where,

A = Assumed mean

f = frequency

d = deviation from the assumed mean

i = Class interval

b. Standard Deviation

$$\text{Standard Deviation, SD } (\sigma) = \sqrt{\frac{\sum fd^2}{N} - \left[\frac{\sum fd}{N}\right]^2} \times i$$

Where,

f = Frequency

d = Deviation from the assumed mean

I = Class interval

N = Total frequency

c. 'T' TEST

To continue the significance of difference between means of various measures test is used: 't' ratio is calculated from the relation.

$$\text{T-ratio} = \frac{M_1 \sim M_2}{\sqrt{\frac{\sigma_1^2}{N_1} + \frac{\sigma_1^2}{N_2}}} = \frac{M_1 \sim M_2}{S \in D}$$

Where,

M_1 M_2 = Means of the groups

SED = Standard Error Deviation

d. F-TEST

F- ratio = Variance between the group / Variance within the group Correlation term

$$C = \frac{\sum x_1 + \sum x_2 + \sum x_3}{N}$$

$$\text{BSS} = \left(\sum x_1\right)^2 / W_1 + \left(\sum x_2\right)^2 / W_2 + \left(\sum x_3\right)^2 W_3 - C$$

$$\text{TSS} = \sum x_1^2 + \sum x_2^2 + \sum x_3^2 - C$$

WSS = TSS - BSS

Where,

$x_1, x_2, x_3,$ are score in different group

C = Correction Terms

TSS = Total Sum of Squares

BSS = Between Sum of Squares

WSS = Within Sum of Squares

e. Co-Efficient of Correlation (R)

$$r = \frac{N\sum x\sum y - \sum x\sum y}{\sqrt{\left(N\sum x^2 - \left(\sum x^2\right)\right)\left(N\sum y^2 - \left(\sum y\right)^2\right.}}$$

x, y – Variables,

N – Total strength.

CONCLUSION

Adopting the methods and the procedures discussed earlier in this chapter tests were administered and marked. This chapter outlined the design of the study, the procedure followed and the nature of the sample. It describes the hypotheses to be tested, selection of tools, and the method of administration and scoring procedures. The obtained data were then analyzed using appropriate statistical techniques. The next chapter presents the analysis and interpretation of the data collected in the light of the hypothesis formulated.

❒

4

Statistical Analysis and Findings

Research consists of systematic observation and description of the characteristic of properties for the purpose of discovering relationships, starts with the description of the measures of the variables and goes on to the higher levels of statistical analysis. The data collected will be carefully edited, systematically classified and tabulated, scientifically analyzed and interpreted and rationally concluded.

Thus, in the present study, the data were collected with regard to Mental Imagery and Academic Stress. The data have been subjected to the following statistical analysis, namely percentile, descriptive, differential, correlation and association. The results of the statistical analysis have been summarized and tabulated.

For the investigator, analysis of collected data turns out to be a very important task. The information collected through the tools have been quantified as detailed in the following tables. For deciding the Academic Stress of the higher secondary school students with respect to Mental Imagery, the following tables were prepared.

CARTEGORISATION OF THE SAMPLE BASED ON THE VARIABLES OF THE STUDY

Categories of the Sample based on Mental Imagery

The sample has been classified on the basis of their Mental Imagery into their three categories (Low, Moderate and High), as indicated in the following tables.

TABLES.4.1: showing the level of Mental Imagery among Higher Secondary School Students

Variable	Number of sample	Range	Level	No of Students	Percentage %
Mental Imagery	348	Below 264	Low	89	25.6
		265 to 328	Moderate	17	49.1
		Above 329	High	88	25.3

INFERENCE

From the table, it is clear that the level of Mental Imagery among higher secondary school students is moderate in nature.

Hence hypothesis 1 stating that "The level of Mental Imagery among the higher secondary school students is moderate in nature" is accepted.

Categories of the sample based on Academic Stress

The Higher secondary school students has been classified on the basis of their Academic Stress into three categories (Low, Moderate and High), as indicated in the table given below.

TABLE.4.2: Showing the level of Academic Stress among the Higher Secondary School Students

Variable	Number of sample	Range	Level	No of Students	Percentage %
Academic Stress	348	Below 264	Low	87	25.6
		265 to 328	Moderate	171	49.1
		Above 329	High	90	25.3

INFERENCE

From the above table, it is found that the level of Academic Stress among the Higher Secondary School Students is moderate in nature.

Hence hypotheses - 2 stating that "The level of Academic stress among higher secondary school students is moderate in nature" is accepted.

INFLUENCE OF GENDER ON VISUAL DIMENSION OF MENTAL IMAGERY

The scores related to Visual dimension of Mental Imagery of Male and Female Higher Secondary School Students have been computed and details are furnished in the following table.

TABLE.4.3: Showing the Significant Difference between the mean Scores of Visual Dimension of Mental Imagery with Respect to Gender

Variable	Gender	N	Mean	S.D	Critical Ratio	L.S
Visual Dimension of Mental Imagery	Boys	173	52.51	10.487	0.021	N.S
	Girls	175	52.49	9.903		

INFERENCE

From the above table, it is clear that the obtained C. R (0.021) value is lower than the table value (1.96) at (0.05) level. Therefore there is no significant difference between the mean scores of visual dimension of Mental Imagery among Higher Secondary School Students with regard to Gender.

Hence the null hypothesis stating that, There is no significant difference between the mean scores of visual dimension of Mental Imagery among Higher Secondary School Students with respect to Gender is accepted.

INFLUENCE OF MEDIUM OF INSTRUCTION ON VISUAL DIMENSION OF MENTAL IMAGERY

The scores related to visual dimension of Mental Imagery of Tamil and English Higher Secondary School Students have been computed and details are furnished in the following table.

TABLE.4.4: Showing the Significant Difference between the mean Scores of Visual Dimension of Mental Imagery with Respect to Medium of Instruction

Variable	Medium of Instruction	N	Mean	S.D	Critical Ratio	L.S
Visual dimension of Mental Imagery	Tamil	123	50.01	10.945	3.423	0.01
	English	225	53.86	9.493		

INFERENCE

From the above table, it is clear that the obtained C. R (3.423) value is lower than the table value (2.58) at (0.01) level. Therefore there is no significant difference between the mean scores of visual dimension of Mental Imagery among Higher Secondary School Students with regard to Gender.

Hence the null hypothesis stating that, There is no significant difference between the mean scores of visual dimension of Mental Imagery among Higher Secondary School Students with respect to Gender is rejected.

INFLUENCE OF TYPE OF MANAGEMENT ON VISUAL DIMENSION OF MENTAL IMAGERY

The scores related to visual dimension of Mental Imagery of Government, Government- Aided and Private of Higher Secondary School Students have been computed and details are furnished in the following table.

TABLE.4.5: ANOVA Showing the Significant Difference between the mean Scores of Visual Dimension of Mental Imagery with Respect to Type of Management

Variable		Sum of Squares	df	Mean Squares	'F' Value	L.S
Visual dimension of Mental Imagery	Between Groups	802.286	2	401.143	3.934	0.05
	Within Groups	35178.711	345	101.967		
	Total	35980.990	347			

INFERENCE

From the table, it is clear that the obtained 'F' value (3.934) is greater than the table value (3.03) at 0.05 level. Therefore there is no significant difference between the mean scores of visual dimension of Mental Imagery among Higher Secondary School Students with regards to Type of Management.

Hence the null hypothesis stating that, There is no significant difference between the mean scores of visual dimension of Mental Imagery among Higher Secondary School Students with respect to Type of Management is accepted.

TABLE.4.5 (A): Showing the Mean, S.D and C.R value for visual Dimension of Mental Imagery of Higher Secondary School Students based on Type of Management

Variable	Type of Management	F	Mean	Std Deviation	C.R Value	L.O.S
Visual dimension of Mental Imagery	Govt. Vs Govt Aided	119	50.45	11.544	1.943	N.S
		109	53.12	8.937		
	Govt Aided Vs Private	109	53.12	8.937	0.692	N.S
		120	53.97	9.539		
	Private Vs Govt	120	53.97	9.539	2.571	0.05
		119	50.45	11.544		

INFERENCE

From the above table following inference have been made.

- In the first case, the calculated C.R value (1.943) is lower than table value (1.96) at 0.05 level of significance, show that there is no significant difference between students studying in Govt and Govt Aided of higher secondary school with respect to visual dimension of Mental Imagery.
- In the second case, the calculated C.R value (0.692) is lower than the table value (1.96) at 0.05 level of significance, show that there is significant difference between students studying in Govt Aided and Private of higher secondary school with respect to visual dimension of Mental Imagery.
- In the third case, the calculated C.R value (2.571) is higher than the expected table value (1.96) at 0.05 level of significance, shows that there is significant difference between students studying in Private and Govt higher secondary school students with respect to visual dimension of Mental Imagery.Hence, the null hypothesis 4 is partially verified.

INFLUENCE OF TYPE OF FAMILY ON VISUAL DIMENSION OF MENTAL MAGERY

The scores related to visual dimension of Mental Imagery of Nuclear and Joint Higher Secondary School Students have been computed and details are furnished in the following table.

TABLE.4.6: Showing the Significant Difference between the mean Scores of visual Dimension of Mental Imagery with Respect to Type of Family

Variable	Type of Family	N	Mean	S.D	Critical Ratio	L.S
Visual Dimension of Mental Imagery	Nuclear	251	51.87	10.152	0.574	N.S
	Joint	97	54.12	10.134		

INFERENCE

From the table, it is clear that the obtained C. R (0.574) value is lower than the table value (1.96) at 0.05 level. Therefore Joint family students have high significant difference of visual dimension of Mental Imagery than Nuclear Family students.

Hence the null hypothesis stating that, There is no significant difference between the mean scores of visual dimension of Mental Imagery among Higher Secondary School Students with respect to Medium of Instruction is accepted.

INFLUENCE OF BIRTH ORDER ON VISUAL DIMENSION OF MENTAL IMAGERY

The scores related to Mental Imagery of 1st / 2nd and Above of Higher Secondary School Students have been computed and details are furnished in the following table.

TABLE.4.7: ANOVA Showing the Significant Difference between the mean Scores of Mental Imagery with Respect to Birth Order

Variable		Sum of Squares	df	Mean Squares	'F' Value	L.S
Visual Dimension of Mental Imagery	Between Groups	5.287	2	2.644	.025	N.S
	Within Groups	35975.710	345	104.277		
	Total	**35980.997**	**347**			

INFERENCE

From the table, it is clear that the obtained 'F' value (0.025) is lower than the table value (3.03) at 0.05 level. Therefore there is no significant difference between the mean scores of visual dimension of Mental Imagery among Higher Secondary School Students regards to Birth Order.

Hence the null hypothesis stating that ,There is no significant difference between the mean scores of visual dimension of Mental Imagery among Higher Secondary School Students with respect to Birth Order is accepted.

INFLUENCE OF GENDER ON AUDITORY DIMENSION OF MENTAL IMAGERY

The scores related to Auditory dimension of Mental Imagery of Male and Female Higher Secondary School Students have been computed and details are furnished in the following table.

TABLE.4.8: Showing the Significant Difference between the mean Scores of Auditory Dimension of Mental Imagery with Respect to Gender

Variable	Gender	N	Mean	S.D	Critical Ratio	L.S
Auditory dimension of Mental Imagery	Male	173	49.77	12.684	1.717	0.05
	Female	175	47.55	11.416		

INFERENCE

From the table, it is clear that the obtained C. R (1.717) value is lower than the table value (1.96) at 0.05 level. Therefore Male students have high significant difference of Auditory dimension of Mental Imagery than Female higher secondary school students.

Hence the null hypothesis stating that, There is no significant difference between the mean scores of auditory dimension of Mental Imagery among Higher Secondary School Students with respect to Gender is accepted.

INFLUENCE OF MEDIUM ON INSTRUCTION IN AUDITORY DIMENSION OF MENTAL IMAGERY

The scores related to Auditory dimension of Mental Imagery of Tamil and English Higher Secondary School Students have been computed and details are furnished in the following table.

TABLE.4.9: Showing the Significant Difference between the mean Scores of Auditory Dimension of Mental Imagery with Respect to Medium of Instruction

Variable	Medium of Instruction	N	Mean	S.D	Critical Ratio	L.S
Auditory Dimension of Mental Imagery	Tamil	123	49.04	12.948	0.442	N.S
	English	225	48.44	11.630		

INFERENCE

From the table, it is clear that the obtained C. R value (0.442) is lower than the table value (1.96) at 0.05 level. Therefore Tamil medium students have high significant difference of auditory dimension of Mental Imagery than English Medium students.

Hence the null hypothesis stating that ,There is no significant difference between the mean scores of auditory dimension of Mental Imagery among Higher Secondary School Students with respect to Medium of Instruction is accepted.

INFLUENCE OF TYPE OF MANAGEMENT ON AUDITORY DIMENSION OF MENTAL IMAGERY

The scores related to Auditory dimension of Mental Imagery of Government, Government- Aided and Private of Higher Secondary School Students have been computed and details are furnished in the following table.

TABLE.4.10: ANOVA Showing the Significant Difference between the mean Scores of Auditory Dimension of Mental Imagery with Respect to Type of Management

Variable		Sum of Squares	df	Mean Squares	'F' Value	L.S
Auditory Dimension of Mental Imagery	Between Groups	227.142	2	113.571	0.775	N.S
	Within Groups	50551.786	345	146.527		
	Total	50778.928	347			

INFERENCE

From the table, it is clear that the obtained 'F' value (0.775) is lower than the table value (3.03) at 0.05 level. Therefore there is no significant difference between the mean scores of auditory dimension of Mental Imagery among Higher Secondary School Students regards to Type of Management.

Hence the null hypothesis stating that, There is no significant difference between the mean scores of auditory dimension of Mental Imagery among Higher Secondary School Students with respect to Type of Management is accepted.

INFLUENCE OF TYPE OF FAMILY ON AUDITORY DIMENSION OF MENTAL IMAGERY

The scores related to Auditory dimension of Mental Imagery of Nuclear and Joint Higher Secondary School Students have been computed and details are furnished in the following table.

TABLE.4.11: Showing the Significant Difference between the mean Scores of Auditory Dimension of Mental Imagery with Respect to Type of Family

Variable	Type of Family	N	Mean	S.D	Critical Ratio	L.S
Auditory Dimension of Mental Imagery	Nuclear	251	48.75	12.309	0.230	N.S
	Joint	97	48.41	11.590		

INFERENCE

From the table, it is clear that the obtained C. R value (0.230) is lower than the table value (1.96) at 0.05 level. Therefore there is no significant difference between the mean scores of auditory dimension of Mental Imagery among Higher Secondary School Students regards to Medium of Instruction.

Hence the null hypothesis stating that, There is no significant difference between the mean scores of auditory dimension of Mental Imagery among Higher Secondary School Students with respect to Medium of Instruction is accepted.

INFLUENCE OF BIRTH ORDER ON AUDITORY DIMENSION OF MENTAL IMAGERY

The scores related to Auditory dimension of Mental Imagery of 1st / 2nd and Above of Higher Secondary School Students have been computed and details are furnished in the following table.

TABLE.4.12: ANOVA Showing the Significant Difference between the mean Scores of Auditory Dimension of Mental Imagery with Respect to Birth Order

Variable		Sum of Squares	df	Mean Squares	'F' Value	L.S
Auditory Dimension of Mental Imagery	Between Groups	26.367	2	13.184	0.090	N.S
	Within Groups	50752.561	345	147.109		
	Total	**50778.928**	**347**			

INFERENCE

From the table, it is clear that the obtained 'F' value (0.090) is lower than the table value (3.03) at 0.05 level. Therefore 1st, 2nd and above students within group is high significant difference of auditory dimension of Mental Imagery than within groups students.

Hence the null hypothesis stating that, There is no significant difference between the mean scores of auditory dimension of Mental Imagery among Higher Secondary School Students with respect to Birth Order is accepted.

INFLUENCE OF GENDER ON GUSTATORY DIMENSION OF MENTAL IMAGERY

The scores related to Gustatory dimension of Mental Imagery of Male and Female Higher Secondary School Students have been computed and details are furnished in the following table.

TABLE.4.13: Showing the Significant Difference between the mean Scores of Gustatory Dimension of Mental Imagery with Respect to Gender

Variable	Gender	N	Mean	S.D	Critical Ratio	L.S
Gustatory Dimension of Mental Imagery	Male	173	54.12	11.991	1.742	N.S
	Female	175	51.99	10.684		

INFERENCE

From the table, it is clear that the obtained C. R value (1.742) is lower than the table value (1.96) at 0.05 level. Therefore Male Students have high significant difference in the gustatory dimension of Mental Imagery than Female Students.

Hence the null hypothesis stating that, There is no significant difference between the mean scores of gustatory dimension of Mental Imagery among Higher Secondary School Students with respect to Gender is accepted.

INFLUENCE ON MEDIUM OF INSTRUCTION IN GUSTATORY DIMENSION OF MENTAL IMAGERY

The scores related to Gustatory Dimension of Mental Imagery of Tamil and English Higher Secondary School Students have been computed and details are furnished in the following table.

TABLE.4.14: Showing the Significant Difference between the mean Scores of Gustatory Dimension of Mental Imagery with Respect to Medium of Instruction

Variable	Medium of Instruction	N	Mean	S.D	Critical Ratio	L.S
Gustatory Dimension of Mental Imagery	Tamil	123	52.04	12.515	1.222	N.S
	English	225	53.60	10.708		

INFERENCE

From the table, it is clear that the obtained C. R value (1.222) is lower than the table value (1.96) at 0.05 level. Therefore Tamil Medium Students have high significant difference in the gustatory dimension of Mental Imagery than English Medium Students.

Hence the null hypothesis stating that, There is no significant difference between the mean scores of gustatory dimension of Mental Imagery among Higher Secondary School Students with respect to Medium of Instruction is accepted.

INFLUENCE OF TYPE OF MANAGEMENT ON GUSTATORY DIMENSION OF MENTAL IMAGERY

The scores related to Gustatory Dimension of Mental Imagery of Government, Government-Aided and Private of Higher Secondary School Students have been computed and details are furnished in the following table.

TABLE.4.15: ANOVA Showing the Significant Difference between the mean Scores of Gustatory Dimension of Mental Imagery with Respect to Type of Management

Variable		Sum of Squares	df	Mean Squares	'F' Value	L.S
Gustatory Dimension of Mental Imagery	Between Groups	59.239	2	29.619	0.227	N.S
	Within Groups	44924.931	345	130.217		
	Total	**44984.170**	**347**			

INFERENCE

From the table, it is clear that the obtained 'F' value is lower than the table value (3.03) at 0.05 level. Therefore there is no significant difference between the mean scores of gustatory dimension of Mental Imagery among Higher Secondary School Students with regards to Type of Management.

Hence the null hypothesis stating that, There is no significant difference between the mean scores of gustatory dimension of Mental Imagery among Higher Secondary School Students with respect to Type of Management is accepted.

INFLUENCE OF TYPE OF FAMILY ON GUSTATORY DIMENSION OF MENTAL IMAGERY

The scores related to Gustatory Dimension of Mental Imagery of Nuclear and Joint Higher Secondary School Students have been computed and details are furnished in the following table.

TABLE.4.16: Showing the Significant Difference between the mean Scores of Gustatory Dimension of Mental Imagery with Respect to Type of Family

Variable	Type of Family	N	Mean	S.D	Critical Ratio	L.S
Gustatory Dimension of Mental Imagery	Nuclear	251	53.11	11.808	0.155	N.S
	Joint	97	52.90	10.270		

INFERENCE

From the table, it is clear that the obtained C. R value (0.155) is lower than the table value (1.96) at 0.05 level. Therefore Nuclear Family Students have high significant difference of gustatory dimension of Mental Imagery than Joint Family Students.

Hence the null hypothesis stating that, There is no significant difference between the mean scores of gustatory dimension of Mental Imagery among Higher Secondary School Students with respect to Medium of Instruction is accepted.

INFLUENCE OFBIRTH ORDER ON GUSTATORY DIMENSION OF MENTAL IMAGERY

The scores related to Gustatory Dimension of Mental Imagery of $1^{st}/2^{nd}$ and Above of Higher Secondary School Students have been computed and details are furnished in the following table.

TABLE.4.17: ANOVA Showing the Significant Difference between the mean Scores of Gustatory Dimension of Mental Imagery with Respect to Birth Order

Variable		Sum of Squares	df	Mean Squares	'F' Value	L.S
Gustatory Dimension of Mental Imagery	Between Groups	13.896	2	6.948	0.053	N.S
	Within Groups	44970.273	345	130.349		
	Total	**44984.170**	**347**			

INFERENCE

From the table, it is clear that the obtained 'F' value (0.053) is lower than the table value (3.03) at 0.05 level. Therefore 1st, 2nd and above students within group is high significant difference of gustatory dimension of Mental Imagery than within groups students.

Hence the null hypothesis stating that, There is no significant difference between the mean scores of gustatory dimension of Mental Imagery among Higher Secondary School Students with respect to Birth Order is accepted.

INFLUENCE OF GENDER ON OLFACTORY DIMENSION OF MENTAL IMAGERY

The scores related to Olfactory Dimension of Mental Imagery of Male and Female Higher Secondary School Students have been computed and details are furnished in the following table.

TABLE 4.18: Showing the Significant Difference between the mean Scores of Olfactory Dimension of Mental Imagery with Respect to Gender

Variable	Gender	N	Mean	S.D	Critical Ratio	L.S
Olfactory Dimension of Mental Imagery	Male	173	52.16	13.174	0.195	N.S
	Female	175	51.92	9.698		

INFERENCE

From the table, it is clear that the obtained C. R value (0.195) is lower than the table value (1.96) at 0.05 level. Therefore male students have high significant difference of Olfactory dimension of Mental Imagery than Female Students.

Hence the null hypothesis stating that, There is no significant difference between the mean scores of Olfactory dimension of Mental Imagery among Higher Secondary School Students with respect to Gender is accepted.

INFLUENCE OF MEDIUM OF INSTRUCTION ON OLFACTORY DIMENSION OF MENTAL IMAGERY

The scores related to Olfactory Dimension of Mental Imagery of Tamil and English Higher Secondary School Students have been computed and details are furnished in the following table.

TABLE.4.19: Showing the Significant Difference between the mean Scores of Olfactory Dimension of Mental Imagery with Respect to Medium of Instruction

Variable	Medium of Instruction	N	Mean	S.D	Critical Ratio	L.S
Olfactory Dimension of Mental Imagery	Tamil	123	51.54	13.015	0.592	N.S
	English	225	52.31	10.671		

INFERENCE

From the table, it is clear that the obtained C. R value (0.592) is lower than the table value (1.96) at 0.05 level. Therefore Tamil Medium students have high significant difference of Olfactory dimension of Mental Imagery than English Medium students.

Hence the null hypothesis stating that ,There is no significant difference between the mean scores of Olfactory dimension Mental Imagery among Higher Secondary School Students with respect to Medium of Instruction" is accepted.

INFLUENCE OF TYPE OF MANAGEMENT IN OLFACTORY DIMENSION ON MENTAL IMAGERY

The scores related to factory Dimension ofMental Imagery of Government, Government- Aided and Private of Higher Secondary School Students have been computed and details are furnished in the following table.

TABLE.4.20: ANOVA Showing the Significant Difference between the mean Scores of Olfactory Dimension of Mental Imagery with Respect to Type of Management

Variable		Sum of Squares	df	Mean Squares	'F' Value	L.S
Olfactory Dimension of Mental Imagery	Between Groups	34.334	2	17.167	0.128	N.S
	Within Groups	46185.102	345	133.870		
	Total	**46219.437**	**347**			

INFERENCE

From the table, it is clear that the obtained 'F' value (0.128) is lower than the table value (3.03) at 0.05 level. Therefore within group students have high significant difference of Olfactory dimension of Mental Imagery than between group students.

Hence the null hypothesis stating that, There is no significant difference between the mean scores of Mental Imagery among Higher Secondary School Students with respect to Type of Management is accepted.

INFLUENCE OF TYPE OF FAMILY IN OLFACTORY DIMENSION ON MENTAL IMAGERY

The scores related to Olfactory Dimension of Mental Imagery of Nuclear and Joint Higher Secondary School Students have been computed and details are furnished in the following table.

TABLE.4.21: Showing the Significant Difference between the mean Scores of Olfactory Dimension of Mental Imagery with Respect to Type of Family

Variable	Type of Family	N	Mean	S.D	Critical Ratio	L.S
Olfactory Dimension of Mental Imagery	Nuclear	251	51.87	11.320	0.446	N.S
	Joint	97	52.48	12.144		

INFERENCE

From the table, it is clear that the obtained C. R value (0.446) is lower than the table value (1.96) at 0.05 level. Therefore Joint House students have high significant difference of Olfactory dimension Mental Imagery than Nuclear House students.

Hence the null hypothesis stating that, There is no significant difference between the mean scores of Mental Imagery among Higher Secondary School Students with respect to Medium of Instruction is accepted.

INFLUENCE OF BIRTH ORDER IN OLFACTORY DIMENSION ON MENTAL IMAGERY

The scores related to Olfactory Dimension of Mental Imagery of 1st / 2nd and Above of Higher Secondary School Students have been computed and details are furnished in the following table.

TABLE.4.22: ANOVA Showing the Significant Difference between the mean Scores of Olfactory Dimension of Mental Imagery with Respect to Birth Order

Variable		Sum of Squares	df	Mean Squares	'F' Value	L.S
Olfactory Dimension of Mental Imagery	Between Groups	96.310	2	48.155	0.360	N.S
	Within Groups	46123.127	345	133.690		
	Total	**46219.437**	**347**			

INFERENCE

From the table, it is clear that the obtained 'F' value (0.360) is lower than the table value (3.03) at 0.05 level. Therefore within group students have high significant difference of Olfactory dimension of Mental Imagery than between group students.

Hence the null hypothesi stating that, There is no significant difference between the mean scores of Olfactory dimension of Mental Imagery among Higher Secondary School Students with respect to Birth Order is accepted.

INFLUENCE OF GENDER IN TACTUAL DIMENSION ON MENTAL IMAGERY

The scores related to Tactual Dimension of Mental Imagery of Male and Female Higher Secondary School Students have been computed and details are furnished in the following table.

TABLE.4.23: Showing the Significant Difference between the mean Scores of Tactual Dimension of Mental Imagery with Respect to Gender

Variable	Gender	N	Mean	S.D	Critical Ratio	L.S
Tactual Dimension of Mental Imagery	Male	173	47.41	15.420	2.967	0.01
	Female	175	42.51	15.366		

INFERENCE

From the table, it is clear that the obtained C. R value (2.967) is greater than the table value (2.58) at (0.01) level. Therefore male students have high significant difference of Tactual dimension of Mental Imagery than female students.

Hence the null hypothesis stating that, There is significant difference between the mean scores of Tactual dimension of Mental Imagery among Higher Secondary School Students with respect to Gender is rejected.

INFLUENCE OF MEDIUM OF INSTRUCTION IN TACTUAL DIMENSION ON MENTAL IMAGERY

The scores related to Tactual Dimension of Mental Imagery of Tamil and English Higher Secondary School Students have been computed and details are furnished in the following table.

TABLE.4.24: Showing the Significant Difference between the mean Scores of Tactual Dimension of Mental Imagery with Respect to Medium of Instruction

Variable	Medium of Instruction	N	Mean	S.D	Critical Ratio	L.S
Tactual Dimension of Mental Imagery	Tamil	123	43.27	15.678	1.491	N.S
	English	225	45.87	15.461		

INFERENCE

From the table, it is clear that the obtained C.R value (1.491) is lower than the table value (1.96) at 0.05 level. Therefore English Medium students have high significant difference of Tactual dimension of Mental Imagery than Tamil medium students.

Hence the null hypothesis stating that ,There is no significant difference between the mean scores of Tactual dimension of Mental Imagery among Higher Secondary School Students with respect to Medium of Instruction" is accepted.

INFLUENCE OF TYPE OF MANAGEMENT IN TACTUAL DIMENSION ON MENTAL IMAGERY

The scores related to Tactual Dimension of Mental Imagery of Government, Government- Aided and Private of Higher Secondary School Students have been computed and details are furnished in the following table.

TABLE. 4.25: ANOVA Showing the Significant Difference between the mean Scores of Tactual Dimension of Mental Imagery with Respect to type of Management

Variable		Sum of Squares	df	Mean Squares	'F' Value	L.S
Tactual Dimension of Mental Imagery	Between Groups	654.405	2	327.202	1.353	N.S
	Within Groups	83414.664	345	241.782		
	Total	**84069.069**	**347**			

INFERENCE

From the table, it is clear that the obtained 'F' value (1.353) is greater than the table value (3.03) at 0.05 level. Therefore between group students have high significant difference of Tactual dimension of Mental Imagery than within group students.

Hence the null hypothesis stating that ,There is no significant difference between the mean scores of Tactual dimension of Mental Imagery among Higher Secondary School Students with respect to Type of Management is accepted.

INFLUENCE OF TYPE OF FAMILY ON TACTUAL DIMENSION OF MENTAL IMAGERY

The scores related to Tactual Dimension of Mental Imagery of Nuclear and Joint Higher Secondary School Students have been computed and details are furnished in the following table.

TABLE.4.26: Showing the Significant Difference between the mean Scores of Tactual Dimension of Mental Imagery with respect to Type of Family

Variable	Type of Family	N	Mean	S.D	Critical Ratio	L.S
Tactual Dimension of Mental Imagery	Nuclear	251	44.98	15.539	0.069	N.S
	Joint	97	44.86	15.714		

INFERENCE

From the table, it is clear that the obtained C. R value (0.069) is lower than the table value (1.96) at 0.05 level. Therefore there is no significant difference between the mean scores of Tactual dimension of Mental Imagery among Higher Secondary School Students regards to Type of family.

Hence the null hypothesis stating that, There is no significant difference between the mean scores of Tactual dimension of Mental Imagery among Higher Secondary School Students with respect to Type of Family is accepted.

INFLUENCE OF BIRTH ORDER ON TACTUAL DIMENSION OF MENTAL IMAGERY

The scores related to Tactual Dimension of Mental Imagery of 1st / 2nd and Above of Higher Secondary School Students have been computed and details are furnished in the following table.

TABLE.4.27: ANOVA Showing the Significant Difference between the mean Scores of Tactual Dimension of Mental Imagery with respect to Birth Order

Variable		Sum of Squares	df	Mean Squares	'F' Value	L.S
Tactual Dimension of Mental Imagery	Between Groups	1739.751	2	869.876	3.645	N.S
	Within Groups	82329.319	345	238.636		
	Total	**84069.069**	**347**			

INFERENCE

From the table, it is clear that the obtained 'F' value (3.645) is greater than the table value (3.03) at 0.05 level. Therefore between group students have high significant difference of Tactual dimension of Mental Imagery than within group students.

Hence the null hypothesis stating that,There is no significant difference between the mean scores of Tactual dimension Mental Imagery among Higher Secondary School Students with respect to Birth Order is rejected

INFLUENCE OF GENDER ON BODILY DIMENSION OF MENTAL IMAGERY

The scores related to Bodily dimension of Mental Imagery of Male and Female Higher Secondary School Students have been computed and details are furnished in the following table.

TABLE.4.28: Showing the Significant Difference between the mean Scores of Bodily Dimension of Mental Imagery with Respect to Gender

Variable	Gender	N	Mean	S.D	Critical Ratio	L.S
Bodily dimension of Mental Imagery	Male	173	45.32	16.839	0.530	N.S
	Female	175	46.21	14.305		

INFERENCE

From the table, it is clear that the obtained C. R value (0.530) is lower than the table value (1.96) at 0.05 level of significance. Therefore Male students have high significant difference of bodily dimension of Mental Imagery than Female students.

Hence the null hypothesis, There is no significant difference between the mean scores of bodily dimension of Mental Imagery among Higher Secondary School Students with respect to Gender is accepted.

INFLUENCE OF MEDIUM OF INSTRUCTION ON BODILY DIMENSION OF MENTAL IMAGERY

The scores related to Bodily dimension of Mental Imagery of Tamil and English Higher Secondary School Students have been computed and details are furnished in the following table.

TABLE.4.29: Showing the Significant Difference between the mean Scores of Bodily Dimension of Mental Imagery with Respect to Medium of Instruction

Variable	Medium of Instruction	N	Mean	S.D	Critical Ratio	L.S
Bodily dimension of Mental Imagery	Tamil	123	41.93	18.002	3.438	0.01
	English	225	47.86	13.713		

INFERENCE

From the table, it is clear that the obtained C. R value (3.438) is greater than the table value (4.61) at 0.01 level of significance. Therefore English Medium students have high significant difference of bodily dimension of Mental Imagery than Tamil Medium students.

Hence the null hypothesis , There is no significant difference between the mean scores of bodily dimension of Mental Imagery among Higher Secondary School Students with respect to Medium of Instruction is rejected.

INFLUENCE OF TYPE OF MANAGEMENT ON BODILY DIMENSION OF MENTAL IMAGERY

The scores related to Bodily dimension of Mental Imagery of Government, Government- Aided and Private of Higher Secondary School Students have been computed and details are furnished in the following table.

TABLE.4.30: ANOVA Showing the Significant Difference between the mean Scores of Bodily Dimension of Mental Imagery with Respect to Type of Management

Variable		Sum of Squares	df	Mean Squares	'F' Value	L.S
Bodily dimension of Mental Imagery	Between Groups	360.425	2	180.213	0.739	0.05
	Within Groups	84090.253	345	243.740		
	Total	**84450.678**	**347**			

INFERENCE

From the table, it is clear that the obtained 'F' value (0.739) is lower than the table value (3.03) at 0.05 level. Therefore within group students have high significant difference of bodily dimension of Mental Imagery than between group students.

Hence the null hypothesis stating that, There is no significant difference between the mean scores of bodily dimension of Mental Imagery among Higher Secondary School Students with respect to Type of Management" is accepted.

INFLUENCE OF TYPE OF FAMILY ON BODILY DIMENSION OF MENTAL IMAGERY

The scores related to Bodily dimension of Mental Imagery of Nuclear and Joint Higher Secondary School Students have been computed and details are furnished in the following table.

TABLE.4.31: Showing the Significant Difference between the mean Scores of Bodily Dimension of Mental Imagery with Respect to Type of Family

Variable	Type of Family	N	Mean	S.D	Critical Ratio	L.S
Bodily dimension of Mental Imagery	Nuclear	251	44.87	15.763	1.728	N.S
	Joint	97	48.08	15.005		

INFERENCE

From the table, it is clear that the obtained C.R value (1.728) is lower than the table value (1.96) at 0.05 level. Therefore Joint Family students have high significant difference of bodily dimension of Mental Imagery than Nuclear Family students.

Hence the null hypothesis stating that, There is no significant difference between the mean scores of bodily dimension Mental Imagery among Higher Secondary School Students with respect to Type of Family is accepted.

INFLUENCE OF BIRTH ORDER ON BODILY DIMENSION OF MENTAL IMAGERY

The scores related to Bodily dimension of Mental Imagery of 1st / 2nd and Above of Higher Secondary School Students have been computed and details are furnished in the following table.

TABLE.4.32: ANOVA Showing the Significant Difference between the mean Scores of Bodily Dimension of Mental Imagery with Respect to Birth Order

Variable		Sum of Squares	df	Mean Squares	'F' Value	L.S
Bodily dimension of Mental Imagery	Between Groups	332.165	2	166.082	0.681	N.S
	Within Groups	84118.513	345	243.622		
	Total	**84450.678**	**347**			

INFERENCE

From the table, it is clear that the obtained 'F' value (0.681) is lower than the table value (3.03) at 0.05 level. Therefore there is no significant difference between the mean scores of bodily dimension of Mental Imagery among Higher Secondary School Students regards to Type of Management.

Hence the null hypothesis, There is no significant difference between the mean scores of bodily dimension of Mental Imagery among Higher Secondary School Students with respect to Birth Order is accepted.

INFLUENCE ON GENDER OF ACADEMIC STRESS

The scores related to Academic stress of Male and Female Higher Secondary School Students have been computed and details are furnished in the following table.

TABLE.4.33: Showing the Significant Difference between the mean Scores of Academic Stress with Respect to Gender

Variable	Gender	N	Mean	S.D	Critical Ratio	L.S
Academic Stress	Male	173	114.92	43.717	4.102	0.01
	Female	175	96.29	40.994		

INFERENCE

From the table, it is clear that the obtained C. R value (4.102) is lower than the table value (2.58) at (0.01) level. Therefore Male students have high significant difference of Academic Stress than Female students

Hence the null hypothesis, There is no significant difference between the mean scores of Academic Stress among Higher Secondary School Students with respect to Gender is rejected.

INFLUENCE ON MEDIUM OF INSTRUCTION OF ACADEMIC STRESS

The scores related to Academic Stress of Tamil and English Higher Secondary School Students have been computed and details are furnished in the following table.

TABLE.4.34: Showing the Significant Difference between the mean Scores of Academic Stress with Respect to Medium of Instruction

Variable	Medium of Instruction	N	Mean	S.D	Critical Ratio	L.S
Academic Stress	Tamil	123	101.98	45.595	1.140	N.S
	English	225	107.51	42.007		

INFERENCE

From the table, it is clear that the obtained C.R value (1.140) is lower than the table value (1.96) at 0.05 level. Therefore English Medium students have high significant difference of Academic Stress than Tamil Medium students

Hence the null hypothesis , There is no significant difference between the mean scores of Academic Stress among Higher Secondary School Students with respect to Medium of Instruction is accepted.

INFLUENCE ON TYPE OF MANAGEMENT OF ACADEMIC STRESS

The scores related to Academic Stress of Government, Government-Aided and Private of Higher Secondary School Students have been computed and details are furnished in the following table.

TABLE.4.35: ANOVA Showing the Significant Difference between the mean Scores of Academic Stress with Respect to Type of Management

Variable		Sum of Squares	df	Mean Squares	'F' Value	L.S
Academic Stress	Between Groups	3552.285	2	1776.142	0.946	N.S
	Within Groups	647773.68	345	1877.605		
	Total	**651325.96**	**347**			

INFERENCE

From the table, it is clear that the obtained 'F' value (0.946) is lower than the table value (3.03) at 0.05 level. Therefore there is no significant difference between the mean scores of Academic Stress among Higher Secondary School Students regards to Type of Management.

Hence the null hypothesis , There is no significant difference between the mean scores of Academic Stress among Higher Secondary School Students with respect to Type of Management is accepted.

INFLUENCE ON TYPE OF FAMILY OF ACADEMIC STRESS

The scores related to Academic Stress of Nuclear and Joint Higher Secondary School Students have been computed and details are furnished in the following table.

TABLE.4.36: Showing the Significant Difference between the mean Scores of Academic Stress with Respect to Type of Family

Variable	Type of Family	N	Mean	S.D	Critical Ratio	L.S
Academic Stress	Nuclear	251	102.94	42.596	1.814	0.05
	Joint	97	112.31	44.674		

INFERENCE

From the table, it is clear that the obtained C.R value (1.814) is lower than the table value (1.96) at 0.05 level. Therefore Joint Family students have high significant difference of Academic Stress than Nuclear Family students

Hence the null hypothesis , There is no significant difference between the mean scores of Academic Stress among Higher Secondary School Students with respect to Type of Family is accepted.

INFLUENCE ON BIRTH ORDER OF MENTAL IMAGERY

The scores related to Academic Stress of 1st / 2nd and Above of Higher Secondary School Students have been computed and details are furnished in the following table.

TABLE. 4.37: ANOVA Showing the Significant Difference between the mean Scores of Academic Stress with respect to Birth Order

Variable		Sum of Squares	df	Mean Squares	'F' Value	L.S
Mental Imagery	Between Groups	45.487	2	22.743	0.012	3.03
	Within Groups	651280.48	345	1887.769		
	Total	**651325.96**	**347**			

INFERENCE

From the table, it is clear that the obtained 'F' value (0.012) is lower than the table value (3.03) at 0.05 level. Therefore there is no significant difference between the mean scores of Academic Stress among Higher Secondary School Students regards to Birth Order.

Hence the null hypothesis , There is no significant difference between the mean scores of Academic Stress among Higher Secondary School Students with respect to Birth Order is accepted.

INFLUENCE OF RELATION BETWEEN THE MENTAL IMAGERY AND ACADEMIC STRESS

The scores related to relation correlation between the Mental Imagery and Academic Stress of Higher Secondary School Students have been computed and details are furnished in the following table.

TABLE.4.38: Correlation

Variable	N	'r' Value	L.S
Mental Imagery and Academic Stress	348	.215	0.01

INFERENCE

From the above table, it is clearly observed that the 'r' value (0.215) is greater than the table value (0.148) 0.01 level. So there is significant correlation between Mental Imagery and Academic Stress among higher secondary school students.

Hence the null hypothesis, there is significant correlation between Mental Imagery and Academic stress among higher secondary school; students is rejected."

CONCLUSION

This chapter summarizes that analysis data, test of hypothesis description and inferences of the tables. A brief report of the research study together with the major finding and conclusion along with their educational implication has been presented in the succeeding chapter.

❒

5

Summary, Findings and Conclusion

This chapter deals with the consolidation of the various findings presented in the previous chapter. Findings are statements of factual information based upon data analysis. Conclusion is answers to the questions raised or the statements of acceptance or rejection of the hypotheses proposed. In this chapter the researcher deals with the aspects pertaining to the tools used for the investigations, objectives and hypotheses of the study, based on analysis the major findings arrived at, and all finally the educational implication together with suggestion for further research. The aim of the present investigation is to study mental imagery and academic stress among higher secondary school students.

STATEMENT OF THE PROBLEM

"Mental Imagery and Academic Stress of Higher Secondary School Students"

OBJECTIVES OF THE STUDY

1. To find out the level of mental imagery among higher secondary school students.
2. To find out the level of academic stress among the higher secondary school students.
3. To find out the significant difference in mental imagery along with its dimensions among the higher secondary school students with respect to
   - Gender
   - Medium of Instruction
   - Type of Management
   - Type of Family
   - Birth Order
4. To find out the significant difference in academic stress among the higher secondary school students with respect on to
   - Gender
   - Medium of Instruction
   - Type of Management
   - Type of Family
   - Birth Order
5. To find out the significant relationship between mental imagery and its dimension and academic stress among the higher secondary school students.
6. To find out the significant correlation between mental imagery and academic stress among the higher secondary school students

HYPOTHESES OF THE STUDY

The following hypotheses have been framed by the researcher for the present study.

1. The levels of mental imagery of higher secondary school students are moderate in nature.
2. The level of academic stress of higher secondary school students is moderate in nature.
3. There is no significant difference in the visual dimension of mental imagery among higher secondary school students with respect to
   - Gender
   - Medium of Instruction
   - Type of Management
   - Type of Family
   - Birth Order

4. There is no significant difference in the Auditory dimension of mental imagery among higher secondary school students with respect to
    - Gender
    - Medium of Instruction
    - Type of Management
    - Type of Family
    - Birth Order
5. There is no significant difference in the Gustatory dimension of mental imagery among higher secondary school students with respect to
    - Gender
    - Medium of Instruction
    - Type of Management
    - Type of Family
    - Birth Order
6. There is no significant difference in the Olfactory dimension of mental imagery among higher secondary school students with respect to
    - Gender
    - Medium of Instruction
    - Type of Management
    - Type of Family
    - Birth Order
7. There is no significant difference in the Tactual dimension of mental imagery among higher secondary school students with respect to
    - Gender
    - Medium of Instruction
    - Type of Management
    - Type of Family
    - Birth Order
8. There is no significant difference in the Bodily dimension of mental imagery among higher secondary school students with respect to
    - Gender
    - Medium of Instruction
    - Type of Management
    - Type of Family
    - Birth Order
9. There is no significant difference of academic stress among higher secondary school students with respect to

- Gender
- Medium of Instruction
- Type of Management
- Type of Family
- Birth Order

10. There is no significant relation between the mental imagery and academic stress of higher secondary school students.
11. There is no significant correlation between mental imagery and academic stress of higher secondary school students.

SAMPLE OF THE STUDY

Data was collected from the higher secondary students adopting stratified random sampling method. The total sample size was 348 drawn from four of schools which were selected for the study belonging to different types of Management: *Government, Government Aided and Private* schools.

TOOLS USED BY THE INVESTIGATOR

To test the hypotheses formulated, the following tools have been used in the present study.

1. Personal data sheet developed by the investigator.
2. Mental Imagery developed and standardized by Dr.M.Rajamanickam was adopted
3. Academic Stress developed and Standardized by S. Mani. (2012) adopted

MAJOR FINDINGS

Based on the analysis of the data, the major findings are listed below.

1. The level of Mental Imagery and its dimension among Higher Secondary School Students is moderate in nature.
2. The level of Academic Stress among Higher Secondary School Students is moderate in nature.
3. Male and female students of Higher Secondary School do not differ significantly in visual dimension of Mental Imagery with regards to Gender.
4. English Medium and Tamil Medium higher secondary school students differ significantly in visual dimension of Mental Imagery with regards to Medium of instruction.
5. Government, Government Aided and Private of higher secondary school students differ significantly in visual dimension of Mental Imagery with regards to Type of Management.

6. Nuclear and Joint Family of higher secondary school students do not differ significantly in visual dimension of Mental Imagery with regards to Type of Family.
7. Male and female students of Higher Secondary School do not differ significantly in visual dimension of Mental Imagery with regards to Birth Order.
8. Male and female students of Higher Secondary School do not differ significantly in auditory dimension of Mental Imagery with regards to Gender
9. English Medium and Tamil Medium higher secondary school students do not differ significantly in auditory dimension of Mental Imagery with regards to Medium in instruction.
10. Government, Government Aided and Private of higher secondary school students do not differ significantly in auditory dimension of Mental Imagery with regards to Type of Management.
11. Nuclear and Joint Family of higher secondary school students do not differ significantly in auditory dimension of Mental Imagery with regards to Type of Family.
12. Male and female students of Higher Secondary School do not differ significantly in auditory dimension of Mental Imagery with regards to Birth Order.
13. Male and female students of Higher Secondary School do not differ significantly in gustatory dimension of Mental Imagery with regards to Gender.
14. English Medium and Tamil Medium higher secondary school students do not differ significantly in gustatory dimension of Mental Imagery with regards to Medium in instruction.
15. Government, Government Aided and Private of higher secondary school students do not differ significantly in gustatory dimension of Mental Imagery with regards to Type of Management.
16. Nuclear and Joint Family of higher secondary school students do not differ significantly in gustatory dimension of Mental Imagery with regards to Type of Family.
17. Male and female students of Higher Secondary School do not differ significantly in gustatory dimension of Mental Imagery with regards to Birth Order.
18. Male and female students of Higher Secondary School do not differ significantly in olfactory dimension of Mental Imagery with regards to Gender.

19. English Medium and Tamil Medium higher secondary school students do not differ significantly in olfactory dimension of Mental Imagery with regards to Medium in instruction.
20. Government, Government Aided and Private of higher secondary school students do not differ significantly in olfactory dimension of Mental Imagery with regards to Type of Management.
21. Nuclear and Joint Family of higher secondary school students do not differ significantly in olfactory dimension of Mental Imagery with regards to Type of Family.
22. Male and female students of Higher Secondary School do not differ significantly in olfactory dimension of Mental Imagery with regards to Birth Order.
23. Male and female students of Higher Secondary School differ significantly in Tactual dimension of Mental Imagery with regards to Gender.
24. English Medium and Tamil Medium higher secondary school students do not differ significantly in Tactual dimension of Mental Imagery with regards to Medium in instruction.
25. Government, Government Aided and Private of higher secondary school students do not differ significantly in Tactual dimension of Mental Imagery with regards to Type of Management.
26. Nuclear and Joint Family of higher secondary school students do not differ significantly in Tactual dimension of Mental Imagery with regards to Type of Family.
27. Male and female students of Higher Secondary School do not differ significantly in Tactual dimension of Mental Imagery with regards to Birth Order.
28. Male and female students of Higher Secondary School do not differ significantly in bodily dimension of Mental Imagery with regards to Gender.
29. English Medium and Tamil Medium higher secondary school students differ significantly in bodily dimension of Mental Imagery with regards to Medium in instruction.
30. Government, Government Aided and Private of higher secondary school students do not differ significantly in bodily dimension of Mental Imagery with regards to Type of Management.
31. Nuclear and Joint Family of higher secondary school students do not differ significantly in bodily dimension of Mental Imagery with regards to Type of Family.

32. Male and female students of Higher Secondary School do not differ significantly in bodily dimension of Mental Imagery with regards to Birth Order.
33. Male and female students of Higher Secondary School do not differ significantly in Academic stress with regards to Gender
34. English Medium and Tamil Medium higher secondary school students do not differ significantly in Academic stress with regards to Medium in instruction.
35. Government, Government Aided and Private of higher secondary school students do not differ significantly in Academic stress with regards to Type of Management.
36. Nuclear and Joint Family of higher secondary school students do not differ significantly in Academic stress with regards to Type of Family
37. Male and female students of Higher Secondary School do not differ significantly in Academic stress with regards to Birth Order.
38. There is no significant correlation between mental imagery and academic stress of higher secondary school students.

EDUCATIONAL IMPLICATIONS & RECOMMENDATIONS

The findings of the present investigation are important for the improvement in the Quality of education, Mental Imagery being an important aspect of human behaviour throws light on the behaviour of the higher secondary school students. Mental Imagery is also an ability which plays a major role in life.

Parents could be the proper motivator to develop mental imagery among the higher secondary school students through the process of guiding, directing, stimulating arid encouraging at every step.

Most of the programmes in school are heavily oriented towards information sharing rather than encouraging and developing Mental Imagery. Therefore it is a felt need to review and modify the programmes in school.

Mental Imagery helps the students to improve their self or worth value and develop the right attitude towards society and this in future would help them become better persons. This positive attitude automatically increases their achievement level. This increase in Mental Imagery also helps the students to mould themselves into a better personality.

This further help those to be flexible with their friends and fellow beings which pave the way for unity in diversity .Since teachers play a vital role in the development process of any individual, early identification and environment stimulation related to Mental Imagery can be provided. The teachers should adopt modern teaching strategies and methods in the class room to give opportunities required for the enhancement of these qualities could be developed

By organizing workshops, conference, seminars and also including the aspect within the curriculum among the schools.

Development of Mental Imagery among school students is a different complex task. In schools there should be lot of scope for participation in different programmes, curricular and co-curricular activities. Children should be encouraged to participate in all programmes, since they offer scope for developing Flexibility in managing their life, tolerance and self evaluation ability among the individuals.

Academic stress among high secondary school students is found to be high among today's generation because of academic competition faced by the students.

The inter-disciplinary subject are varied and multiple in number these days. This also gives academic stress to higher secondary school students, assumption they are confused in choosing the right option for the career. Teachers also sometimes add to this academic stress among the higher secondary school students, because they want the students to achieve higher than their ability. Proper counselling and be given level of higher secondary school students, by teachers and psychologist to help them overcome academic stress.

The examination system also is so theoretical that many students are academically stressed due to large portion of subject matter to be reproduced.

Parents also play a vital part in building up the students attitude, motivation and interest in their academic from their young age. When the students reach the higher secondary school level in education most of the parents are also equally stressed thinking about the achievement of their own children. This stress is transmitted to the children at this higher secondary school level as academic stress.

The society at large also gives its input in moulding the citizens of tomorrow by way of providing the right environment and role models.

The teachers, parents and the society should be in a position to provide help to the higher secondary school students to lower their academic stress in order to achieve high.

Academic Stress among the students may also be attributed to Academic work load which is high on the students. Sometimes the incapability to cope up with such pressure may also be a cause for the lowering of the mental imagery among them.

The teachers can train the students with various coping strategies, which can help the students to overcome their academic stress.

The students can be given physical activities like performing physical exercise, involving them in a few games etc. which can serve as stress busters.

Teachers can provide necessary counselling to the first generation learners and low achievers which can increase their academic performance and reduce the level of their academic stress. The goal of the school should be to better academic achievement and aspiration among the higher secondary school students to meet up to the challenges they would face in later life.

DELIMITATION OF THE STUDY

This investigation has the following delimitation

1. The sample is limited to 348 students
2. The sample is taken only from Chennai, in Tamil Nadu
3. The sample is higher secondary school students only

The sample are taken only from 1 Government School, 1 Government Aided School, 2 Matriculation School

SUGGESTIONS FOR FURTHER RESEARCH

Following are some of the suggestion put forward by the investigator for further research

1. This study was confirmed with Tamil and English medium higher secondary school students. To make the finding of the study more universal, a comprehensive study of this type involving different standards of students at various levels could be under taken.
2. The study was conducted only in a few selected schools in Chennai, Tamil Nadu. It can be extended to many other schools and in many districts.
3. A comprehensive study can be undertaken among primary, high school, higher secondary school and college students.
4. The study could also be tested on different scholastic groups.
5. The study could also be tested on different groups.

CONCLUSION

The purpose of the study was to study the relationship among the variables viz., Mental Imagery and Academic Stress. The study is sure to find some usefulness in the field of education and findings of the study can serve as a database for future research.

❐

6

The Problem and its Perspectives

"Man is a social animal". This is an early saying of our ancestors; even this statement reveals that man is mainly dependent on his 'Society'. Thorndike defines "Social Intelligence as the ability to understand others and act wisely in human relations. It is the human capacity to understand what is happening in the world and responding to that understanding in a personally and socially effective manner".

The level of intelligence differs among individuals. There are many factors affecting intelligence level as external and internal factors.The subjective happiness is also one of the important factors affecting social intelligence. Higher Secondary students belong to the age of adolescence. Adolescence is a period of social awakening. Through this research work the researcher can analyze the Social Intelligence of higher secondary students in relation to their subjective happiness.

Subjective well-being (SWB) is the scientific term for happiness. People's levels of subjective well- being are influenced by both internal factors, such as personality, outlook, and external factors, such as the society in which they live. Some of the major determinants of subjective well-being are a person's inborn temperament, the quality of their social relationship, the societies they live in, and their ability to meet their basic needs.

Importantly, researches have also studied the outcomes of Subjective well-being and have found that **"happy"** people are more likely to be healthier and live longer, to have better social relationships, and to be more productive at work. Every human needs knowledge about ***Social Intelligence** and* S***ubjective Happiness*** for leading a very beautiful and healthy life in this world.

The present study takes a position that Social Intelligence and Subjective Happiness are very important to the student who lives and grows in the complex social environment. Hence there is a need to find out if there is any correlation between Social Intelligence and Subjective Happiness. Hence the problem merged to study the two variables Social Intelligence and Subjective Happiness.

STATEMENT OF THE PROBLEM

The title of the problem is as follows:

A Critical Study on Social Intelligence of Higher Secondary Students Leading to Their Subjective Happiness.

OPERATIONAL DEFINITIONS

Social Intelligence

Social Intelligence means ability of an individual to react to social situations of daily life. Social Intelligence would not include the feelings or emotions aroused in us by other people, but merely our ability to understand others and to react in such a way towards them that the desired ends should be attained. High Social Intelligence is possessed by those who are able to handle people well. Adequate adjustment in social situations is the index of Social Intelligence.

Definitions of Social Intelligence

E. L. THORNDIKE (1920) has pointed out that there is an aspect of personality that can be called "Social Intelligence", distinct from "concrete" and "abstract" intelligence.

STERNBERY (1984) defines Intelligence as "consisting of purposive selection and shaping of an adaptation to real world environments relevant to one's life".

IMPORTANCE OF SOCIAL INTELLIGENCE

Social Intelligence is at the heart of human happiness and emotional comfort. Explored further, the reason for unhappiness is the inability to maintain positive human relationships with the society. The result will be depression, fear, confusion and anger, created by the lack of positive human emotions that are critical to the happiness of us all. So Social Intelligence is very important in human's life that is created to bring the practical technology of skill based training into the world of human interaction and relations.

NEED FOR SOCIAL INTELLIGENCE

Although anyone can benefit from Social Intelligence training, it has been especially successful with the following group.

- People in high stress job.
- Single or divorced men and women who would like to find and build a healthy relationship.
- Senior-mid level managers.
- Workers in a regular contact with public.

FACTORS OF SOCIAL INTELLIGENCE

The following factors are mostly including in the concept of Social Intelligence.

- Patience
- Co-operativeness
- Confidence Level
- Sensitivity
- Recognitions of Social Environment
- Tactfulness
- Sense of Humour
- Memory

OPERATIONAL DEFINITIONS

Subjective Happiness

Personalized contentment, individual pleasure, emotional satisfaction, subjective-well being and personal enjoyment are some of the synonyms of Subjective Happiness. The term "subjective" itself explains the introspective nature of the variable. Happiness is no laughing matter", says **Richard whately (1954)**.

Diener and **Emmons (1984)** define Subjective Happiness as "an individual's own perception of his/her happiness, which is assessed through ratings of positive of negative effects".

Since the down of civilization great thinkers have discussed the "quality of human existence" and "the good life". Some individuals vary in external circumstance, yet they may share a subjective feeling of well-being.

Definition of Subjective Happiness

Veenhovn (2004) in his content, happiness is commonly understood as how much one likes the life one lives, or more formally, the degree to which one evaluates one's life as a whole.

Matthev killingsworth (2010) happiness is a state of mind or feeling characterized by contentment, love, satisfaction, and pleasure or joy variety of biological, physiological religious and philosophical approaches have striven to define happiness and identify its sources.

MEASURING SUBJECTIVE WELL-BEING

This section presents best practice in measuring subjective well-being. It covers both the range of concepts to be measured and the best approaches for measuring them. This includes considering issues of sample design, survey design, data processing and coding and questionnaire design.

Survey vehicles

Subjective well-being measures are relevant in a wide range of contexts of particular importance for monitoring progress is the inclusion of such measures in integrated household surveys and general social surveys. Time use surveys are the key vehicle for collecting detailed information on affect and its antecedents but it is possible to collect useful information on affect from other household surveys. Measures of subjective well-being are also relevant to victimisation surveys, health Surveys, and special topic surveys. In particular, special topic surveys are excellent vehicles for exploring aspects of subjective well-being in more depth, although they cannot be used to monitor changes in well-being over time due to their "one-off" nature. Including measures of subjective well-being in panel surveys is important for research into causality and the drivers of subjective well-being.

What other information should be collected: Co-variates and analytical and variables

The precise range of co-variates to collect alongside measures of subjective well-being will vary with the specific aspect of subjective well-being that is of interest and with the research question being examined. Despite this, it is possible to present some general guidelines on the most important information that should be collected alongside measures of subjective well-being:

- **Demographics:** Age, gender, marital status (legal marital status and social marital status), family type, number of children, household size, and geographic information.
- **Material Conditions:** Household income, consumption, deprivation, housing quality.

- **Quality of life:** Employment status, health status, work life balance, education and skills, social connections, civic engagement and governance, environmental quality, personal security.
- **Psychological Measures:** aspirations and expectations about the future which forms part of the frame of reference that individuals use when evaluating their lives or reporting their feelings.

Measurement

There is a range of instruments that can be used to measure well-being, although negative/positive affect and cognition are typically measured separately, for example with Bradburn's Affect-Balance Scale and Diener's Satisfaction with Life Scale (SWLS). Measures of SWB vary with the instrument being used. Here is a composite list of factors, with perceptions that people:

1. Find meaning and purpose in life
2. Have sufficient supportive friends and family
3. Support others, sustaining their social capital
4. Have interesting and challenging work
5. Feel competent and able to handle life
6. Are easily amused and smile or laugh often
7. Are good, living by their values
8. Get what they think they deserve
9. Have a positive self-image
10. Feel able to cope with life's emergencies
11. Feel a sense of belonging
12. Have fewer and less intense negative emotions
13. Are optimistic, using much positive language
14. Have basic needs sufficiently satisfied
15. Expect a long, healthy life
16. Do not expect traumatic experiences

Instruments can vary from a few broad questions about happiness or life, to longer lists of more specific items. As with any test, the Holy Grail is to ask the fewest questions that will still give a reliable and valid result.

NEED FOR THE STUDY

Educationalists of the post and present centuries are one, on one point that adolescence is a highly sophisticated stage. Influence of western culture, globalization and media, changed manner and morals in the social growing competition in every field include higher education, career etc. intensities the sophistication that is already associated with adolescence. Pupils who have a self canon and personal cheerfulness can only meet with success in the present scenario.

Subjective well-being (Happiness) is composed of several major components, including global life satisfaction, contentment with specific life domains, the presence of frequent positive affect (pleasant moods and emotions),and a relative absence of negative affect(unpleasant moods and emotions).

From the past decades, inspiration in children had been taken very seriously and they may pretend to be sick and refuse to go to school. As one childhood stage is different from another, it will be difficult to tell whether a child is going through a temporary "phase" or suffering from "mindfulness".

SIGNIFICANCE OF THE STUDY

Happiness is commonly understood as the fundamental goal in life. To create a better society where happiness is ubiquitous, major efforts to understand equality of life is needed. Happiness depends on Social Intelligence. In this study, the Higher Secondary Students who are in a period of stress and storm due to rapid physical changes and at a stage they are forced to choose their career. Their future oriented thinking and their own happiness is important for them in developing their personality and future.

OBJECTIVES OF THE STUDY

The following objectives have been set in the present study.

1. To find out the level of Social Intelligence of Higher Secondary Students.
2. To find out the level of Subjective Happiness of Higher Secondary Students.
3. To find out whether there is any significant difference in Social Intelligence and its dimension among Higher Secondary Students with regard to

Gender	:	Male/Female
Type of Management of Schools	:	Government/ Government Aided
Medium of Instruction	:	Tamil/English
Type of Family	:	Nuclear/Joint
Location of the School	:	Rural/Urban
Birth order	:	First born/Middle born/ Last born

4. To find out whether there is any significant difference in Subjective Happiness among Higher Secondary Students with regard to

Gender	:	Male/Female
Type of Management of Schools	:	Government/ Government Aided schools/Self Finance Schools
Medium of Instruction	:	Tamil/English
Type of Family	:	Nuclear/Joint
Location of the School	:	Rural/Urban
Birth order	:	First born/Middle born/Last born

5. To find out whether there is any significant correlation between Social Intelligence of Higher Secondary Students and their Subjective Happiness.

LIMITATIONS

1. The study was restricted to Thiruvannamalai District of Tamil Nadu.
2. Number of samples was confined to 300.
3. The research is concentrated on three types of schools Government, Government Aided, and Self Finance schools.
4. Only class (+1) level students from Higher Secondary Schools were taken for the study.

CONCLUSION

The chapter dealt with definitions of terms significance and objective and limitations of the present study. Related literature different aspects of this research had been thoroughly reviewed and reported by the researcher in the following chapter.

❐

7

Review of Related Literature

A survey of related studies implies, locating and evaluating reports of relevant researches, study of published articles, research abstracts etc. It orients the readers and serves the following purpose.

It shows whether the evidence already available solves the problem adequately without further investigations and risk of duplication. It provides ideas, theories, explanations or hypotheses valuable in formulating the problem.

It suggests methods of research appropriate to the problem it locates comparative data useful in the interpretation of results. It contributes to the general scholarship of the investigator.

IMPORTANCE OF REVIEW

The importance of the review is well explained by Borg etal (1983) as, "The review to the literature is an important part of the scientific approach and is carried out in all areas of scientific research whether in the physical, natural or social science. It gives the scholars the understanding of previous work that has been done. It provides the means of getting to the frontiers in the particular field of knowledge".

STUDIES RELATED TO SOCIAL INTELLIGENCE

Indian Studies

Dr. Vipinder Nagra (2004) Assistant Professor, D.A.V. College of Education, Hoshiarpur and Punjab, India investigated the Social Intelligence level and Adjustment levels of secondary school students in relation to type of school and gender. Social Intelligence scale and Adjustment Inventory were used for collecting data from a random sample of 200 secondary school students. Statistical techniques such as mean, standard deviations and't' test were applied for analysis of data. The results revealed average levels of Social Intelligence and adjustment in these students. Insignificant differences were observed in Social Intelligence and adjustment in relation to type of school and gender.

R.Lenin (2005) conducted an investigation into Emotional Intelligence and Social Intelligence of teacher's trainee, who were studying under University of Madras. The sample consists of 293 students from 6 teacher training colleges in Chennai. It was found that the level of Social Intelligence and emotional of teacher trainees is moderate in nature and there is a significant relation between Emotional Intelligence and Social Intelligence.

Vootnoori Rajesh (2006) conducted the study, which was analyzing the achievements in social science with related to Emotional Maturity and Social Intelligence of 308 secondary school students in karimnagar district,Andra Pradash. It was found that the level of Emotional Maturity and Social Intelligence of secondary school students is moderate in nature. It was students in that there is significance association between emotional maturity and Social Intelligence.

Dr. Sumanlata Saxena,and Dr. Rajat Kumar Jain (2013) conducted a study on Social Intelligence of male and female undergraduate students of Science and Arts subject streams studying in various degree colleges of Bhilai city, Chhattisgarh. For this purpose descriptive survey method was used. 60 males and 60 females' undergraduate students were selected, for the sample by adopting stratified disproportionate random sampling technique. The data was collected by using Social Intelligence Scale (SIS) constructed and standardized by Chadda and Ganesan (2009). The data was analyzed by using't' test. The findings of gender analysis indicates that female student's posses more Social Intelligence than all students and analysis of stream indicates that arts students are having greater Social Intelligence than students of other streams.

Dr. Rakesh Rail, Meetu Singh (2014) conducted a Study of Social Intelligence among College Students in Relation to their Subject Stream in Bijnor District. The sample consists of male and female undergraduate students of science and Arts subject streams studying in various degree colleges of

Dhampur, Bijnor. Here descriptive survey method was used. 30 Arts and 35 Science undergraduate students were selected, for the sample by adopting stratified disproportionate random sampling technique. The data was collected by using **Social Intelligence Scale (SIS)** constructed and standardized by **Dr. N.K. Chadda** and **Usha Ganesan**. The data was analyzed by using't' test. The findings of gender analysis indicates that female student's posses more Social Intelligence than male students and analysis of stream indicates that arts students are having greater Social Intelligence than students of other streams.

Abroad Studies

Noortjc Mcijs, Antonius H. N. Cillessen, Ron H. J. Scholte, Eliane Segers and Renske Spijkerman(2008) studied on compared the effects of Social Intelligence and Cognitive Intelligence, as measured by academic achievement, on adolescent popularity in two school contexts. A distinction was made between socio metric popularity, a measure of acceptance, and perceived popularity, a measure of social dominance. Participants were 512, 14–15 year-old adolescents (56% girls, 44% boys) in vocational and college preparatory schools in Northwestern Europe. Perceived popularity was significantly related to Social Intelligence, but not to academic achievement, in both contexts. Socio metric popularity was predicted by an interaction between academic achievement and Social Intelligence, further qualified by school context. Whereas college bound students gained socio metric popularity by excelling both socially and academically, vocational students benefited from doing well either socially or academically, but not in combination. The implications of these findings were discussed.

Soleiman Yahyazadeh Jeloudar, Aida Suraya Md Yunus, Samsilah Roslan and Sharifah Md. Nor (2012) investigated the level of Social Intelligence among teachers employed in Government Secondary Schools based on a selected demographic variable. The sample of the study comprised 203 teachers. The findings of the study showed that there was a significant difference among the teachers from (Malaysia, India and China) and their Social Intelligence. The study also revealed that there were significant differences between teachers with high and moderate level of social intelligence in five strategies of classroom discipline used, that is, teachers with high level of Social Intelligence scored higher in the classroom discipline strategies of discussion, recognition, involvement, and hinting, whereas teachers with moderate level of Social Intelligence scored higher in the use of aggression. However, no significant difference was found concerning one strategy of classroom discipline (punishment).

Parto Eshghi, Shahram Arofzad and Taghi Agha Hosaini (2013) investigated the Relationship between Social Intelligence with effective influence among physical education expertise in Isfahan education organizations.Sample consist of 48 physical education expertises in Isfahan education organizations participated in this research. There were 37 men and 11 women, and their ages ranged from 35-46 years-old. To data collection, all subjects filled in the Silvera Social Intelligence Scale (2001) and the Survey of effective influence (SEI). The results showed that the correlation between overall Social Intelligence scores and overall effective influence scores was significant at the level of $P<0.001$. Furthermore, the correlation between overall social intelligence scores and effective influence sub-scales was significant at the level of $P<0.001$. Based on our results, the differences between gender and experience with social intelligence and effective influence were not significant ($P>0.05$) but there was significant difference between academic level and social intelligence ($P<0.05$). Thus, the strength of the correlations obtained in the present research suggests that the overall Social Intelligence has a significant role in effective influence and its sub-scales.

Hassan Aminpoor (2013) Instructor of Psychology, Department of Psychology, Payame Noor University, Tehran, Iran investigated the relationship between Social Intelligence and happiness among male and female university students. 226 students (96 males and 130 females) were selected randomly. Social Intelligence Questionnaire (SIQ) and Oxford Happiness Inventory (OHI) were used to carry out the study. Data analyzed by Pearson correlation coefficient, T test, and ANOVA. The results of the study showed that there is a positive significant relationship between social intelligence and happiness; ANOVA results showed that F value is significant. Thus, it is essential to use post hoc tests. Post hoc test results showed that technical engineering group is higher than basic sciences group in Social Intelligence.

Kamalpreet Kaur Toor (2013) Department of Education and Community Service, Punjabi University, Patiala, India conducted the study on compare Social and Emotional Intelligence among secondary school teachers in relation to gender and type of school. The sample for the study consisted of 850 secondary school teachers of Punjab. The findings of the study revealed there is no significant difference in Social Intelligence of male and female secondary school teachers. Private secondary school teachers being significantly more socially intelligent than government secondary school teachers. These results of main effects of gender and type of school are inter dependent for emotional intelligence, as male secondary school teachers are more emotionally intelligent than female secondary school teachers, only in case of private schools. Government secondary school teachers are more emotionally intelligent than private secondary school teachers, only in case of female group of teachers.

Negin Peyvandi Nezhad,Mansooreh Fazilati,Sodeh Tavakkoli(2014) studied the relationship among Moral Intelligence, Social Intelligence and Self-esteem the students of Central Payam-e-Nour University of Tehran-South. In this research, the expected results were achieved using the three questionnaire named Kil and Jordan's Moral Intelligence questionnaire (2011), Tet's Social Intelligence questionnaire (2008) and Cooper Smith's self-esteem's questionnaire and its distribution among a sample of150 students of Central Payam-e-Nour University of Tehran-South, receiving the information and considering them using the Pearson's correlation coefficient. According to the conducted considerations, the relationship between Moral Intelligence and Social Intelligence is negative and inverse. There is a meaningful relationship between Moral Intelligence and Self-esteem. However, the relationship between Moral Intelligence and general Self-esteem is positive. The conducted considerations indicated that there is a positive and meaningful relationship among each of intelligence and public Self- esteem factors in students. Thus, it can be stated that the amount of Moral Intelligence and Social Intelligence have an influence on students' Self-esteem.

Tayfun Dogan, Faculty of Education, Nigde University and Ali Eryılmaz Faculty of Education, Eskisehir Osmangazi University (2014) conducted a study on the role which Social Intelligence has in Happiness. Two hundred and forty nine university students (130 females/119males) participated in the study. The Turkish Version of the Tromso Social Intelligence Scale (TSIS-TR) and The Turkish Version of the Oxford Happiness Questionnaire Short-Form (OHQ-SF) have been used as data acquisition tools. Pearson Correlation and multiple regression analysis techniques have been used for analyzing data. According to the results of the analysis it has been determined that sub-dimensions of Social Intelligence are positively and statistically significantly related with the Happiness levels of university students. It has been concluded that in terms of the sub-dimensions of Social Intelligence, "social skill" is the dimension that best explains happiness. Social Intelligence explains 16% of the variance in happiness. As a result, Social Intelligence is an important factor for the Happiness of university students.

STUDIES RELATED TO SUBJECTIVE HAPPINESS

Indian Studies

A.Malathi, Asha Damodaran, Nilesh Shah, Neela Patil and Srikrishna Maratha (2004) Mumbai investigated the effect of yogic practices on Subjective Well. Forty eight healthy volunteers who participated in the practice of yoga over a period of 4 months were assessed on Subjective Well Being Inventory (SUB!) before and after the course in order to evaluate the effect of practice of yoga on subjective feelings of well-being and quality of life. A significant improvement in 9 of the 11 factors of SUBI was observed at the end of 4 months, in these participants. The paper thus, reiterates the beneficial effects of regular practice of yoga on Subjective Well Being.

Dr.Debleena Kumar (2004), Assistant Professor, Department of Psychology, Barrackpore Rastraguru Surendranath College, kolkata conducted a study is an attempt to find out the relationship of Stressful Life Events and Happiness in a group of employed adults. Total 100 employed adult individuals (age range 23- 28 years) of both sexes were selected for the present study after an initial screening by General Health Questionnaire-28. To fulfil the objective of the present venture, Oxford Happiness Questionnaire and Presumptive Stressful Life Event Scale were administered on the subjects following a uniform procedure. The nature of relationship was measured by using Pearson"s Product Moment Correlation Coefficient. Results indicated that Stressful Life Events bears a significant negative relationship with Happiness.

Sreekumar. R and Sree Sankaracharya (2008) University of Sanskrit, Kalady, Kerala investigated the pattern of relationship of certain religious aspects, viz., Religious Beliefs, Religious Practices, and Spirituality with Subjective Well Being. The sample of the study consist 350subjects and the tools used were: i. Religious Beliefs Scale, ii. Religious Practices Questionnaire, iii. Spirituality Scale, and iv. Subjective well being Inventory. Statistical techniques such as correlation and path analysis were used for the analysis of data. The results reveal that all the three factors of religious beliefs, religious practices, and spirituality have significant positive correlations with Subjective Well Being. Path analysis yielded a path model and also gave the estimates of the direct, indirect, and total effects of religious beliefs, practices, and spirituality on Subjective Well Being. Spirituality has largest overall effect on Subjective Well Being and the effect of religious beliefs could be interpreted meaningfully considering the intervening variables, i.e., religious practices and spirituality.

Rik Linssen, Luuk van Kempen and Gerbert Kraay kamp(2011) conducted an investigation into Subjective Well-being in Rural India: The Curse of Conspicuous Consumption. Sample consist of 697 individuals from 375 rural low income households in India, we test expectations on the effects of relative income and conspicuous consumption on subjective well-being. The results of the multi-level regression analyses how that individuals who spent more on conspicuous consumption report lower levels of subjective well-being. Surprisingly an individual's relative income position does not affect feelings of well-being. Motivated by positional concerns, people do not passively accept their relative rank but instead consume conspicuous goods to keep up with the Joneses. Conspicuous consumption always comes at the account of the consumption of basic needs. Our analyses point at a positional treadmill effect of the consumption of status goods

Xavier Fontaine and Katsunori Yamada (August 25, 2011) investigated a unique micro-level survey of the relationship between Subjective well-being and Reference Consumption in urban Indian. Using accurate computations of individuals' reference consumption; we find that other's consumption has a positive impact on Subjective well-being. This result validates Hirschman's view that information dominates envy in rapidly developing areas. Whereas envy seems to undermine the well-being impact of growth in economically established countries, growth appears to have an important role in urban Indian. Our finding is robust to the way we define the reference level of consumption.

Abroad Studies

Adrian Furnham and K. V. Petrides (2003), UK conducted a study on measures of trait Emotional Intelligence (trait EI), happiness, personality, and cognitive ability. Neuroticism was negatively related to happiness, whereas Extraversion and Openness to Experience were positively related to it. Cognitive ability was not related either to happiness or to trait EI. A three-step hierarchical regression showed that trait EI explained over 50% of the total variance in happiness. The positive relationship between trait EI and happiness persisted in the presence of the Big Five. In contrast, the Big Five did not account for a significant amount of happiness variance when trait EI was partialled out.

Robert A. Emmons and Michael E. McCullough (2003) investigated the Counting Blessings Versus Burdens: An Experimental Investigation of Gratitude and Subjective Well-Being in Daily Life. The effect of a grateful outlook on psychological and physical well-being was examined. In Studies1and2, participants were randomly assigned to 1 of 3 experimental conditions (hassles, gratitude listing, and either neutral life events or social comparison); they then kept weekly (Study 1) or daily (Study 2) records of their moods, coping behaviours, health behaviours, physical symptoms, and overall life appraisals. In a 3rd study, persons with neuromuscular disease were randomly assigned to either the gratitude condition or to a control condition. The gratitude-outlook groups exhibited heightened well-being across several, though not all, of the outcome measures across the 3 studies, relative to the comparison group's .The effect on positive affect appeared to be the most robust finding. Results suggest that a conscious focus on blessings may have emotional and interpersonal benefits.

Daniel W. Sacks, Betsey Stevenson, JustinWolfers (2010) studied the relationships between Subjective well-being and Income, as seen across individuals within a given country, between countries in a given year, and as a country grows through time. We show that richer individuals in a given country are more satisfied with their lives than are poorer individuals, and establish that this relationship is similar in most countries around the world. Turning to the relationship between countries, we show that average life satisfaction is higher in countries with greater GDP percapita. The magnitude of the satisfaction-income gradient is roughly the same whether we compare individuals or countries, suggesting that absolute income plays an important role in influencing well being .Finally, studying changes in satisfaction over time, we find that as countries experience economic growth, their citizens' life satisfaction typically grows, and that those countries experiencing more rapid economic growth also tend to experience more rapid growth in life satisfaction. These results together suggest that measured Subjective well-being grows hand in hand with material living standards.

Erik Angner (2011) studied the historical roots of Subjective measures of well being, that is, measures designed to represent happiness, satisfaction, or other ,positive or desirable mental states. While it is often suggested that these measures are a modern invention, we argue that they have a long and rich history that conforms to Theodore M. Porter's general account of measurement in social and behavioural science. Subjective measures emerged in marital success studies, educational psychology, and personality psychology in the 1920s and 30s, and were further shaped by the epidemiology of mental health, gerontology, and the social indicator movement in the 1960s and 70s. Consistent with Porter's account, these measures emerged in applied rather than theoretical branches of social and behavioural science, and they did so not as a result of physics envy, but rather as a result of a moral impulse to improve society; quantification was intended to make up for perceived deficiencies in unaided human judgment; and radical disagreements about the nature of well being did not impede efforts to measure it - indeed, in time, there was considerably more agreement about how to measure wellbeing than about how to define it-indeed, in time, there was considerably more agreement about how to measure wellbeing than about how to define it.

Katy W.Y. Liu (2012) investigated the relationship between Humor Styles, Self-esteem and Subjective Happiness among Hong Kong Undergraduate students. 232 undergraduate students from 6 Hong Kong universities are asked to complete a Self-administered questionnaire in the current study. Results showed that males considered themselves as more humorous than females. Meanwhile, males used more aggressive humor styles than females. However, both genders used more adaptive Humor Styles than maladaptive humor styles. Additionally, positive correlations were found between adaptive humor styles,

Self-esteem and Subjective Happiness. Adaptive humor styles were found to strengthen the relationship between Self-esteem and Subjective Happiness. The significant findings on the relationship of humor styles, Self-esteem and Subjective Happiness can be used as reference for similar studies in Hong Kong. In addition, the mediation effects of Humor Styles found in the present research provide useful suggestions for future intervention and therapeutic purposes in promoting mental health.

Robb B. Rutledgea.b, Nikolina Skandalia, Peter Dayanc, and Raymond. J, Dolana.b (2014) investigated a computational and neural model of momentary Subjective well-being. The Subjective well-being or happiness of individuals is an important metric for societies. Although happiness is influenced by life circumstances and population demographics such as wealth, we know little about how the cumulative influence of daily life events are aggregated into Subjective feelings. Using computational modelling, we show that emotional reactivity in the form of momentary happiness in response to outcomes of a probabilistic reward task is explained not by current task earnings, but by the combined influence of recent reward expectations and prediction errors arising from those expectations. The robustness of this account was evident in a large-scale replication involving 18,420 participants. Using functional MRI, we show that the very same influences account for task-dependent striate activity in a manner.

CONCLUSION

The study of related literature has helped the investigator to have a clear perspective of the problem chosen for the present investigation, designing the method of research description of the variable, sample selection of suitable tools administration and scoring methods of responses have been undertaken based on the review which is discussed in the succeeding chapter.

❐

8

Design of the Study

Research design means exact nature of the research work in a systematic measure. It involves the information about the research work in view, of frame work of study, availability of various data, observation, sampling etc.

In any research work, proper selection of the method of investigation is an important step. This requires a careful evaluation of the many standard procedures of collecting data with respect to the objectives of the research programme, a sample on which the study is made, the type of tools used and on different variables. This chapter aims at presenting in detail how the investigation has been planned and carried out.

HYPOTHESES OF THE STUDY

The hypotheses formed in the present study are listed below:

1. The level of Social Intelligence of Higher Secondary Students is average in nature.
2. The level of Subjective Happiness of Higher Secondary Students is average in nature.
3. There is no significant difference in Social Intelligence among Higher Secondary Students with regard to

Gender	:	Male/Female
Type of Management of Schools	:	Government/ Government Aided/Self Finance Schools
Medium of Instruction	:	Tamil/English
Type of Family	:	Nuclear/Joint
Location of the School	:	Rural/Urban
Birth order	:	First born/Middle born/Last born

4. There is no significant difference in Patience - a dimension of Social Intelligence among Higher Secondary Students with regard to

Gender	:	Male/Female
Type of Management of Schools	:	Government/Government Aided /Self Finance Schools
Medium of Instruction	:	Tamil/English
Type of Family	:	Nuclear/Joint
Location of the School	:	Rural/Urban
Birth order	:	First born/Middle born/Last born

5. There is no significant difference in Co - cooperativeness - a dimension of Social Intelligence among Higher Secondary Students with regard to

Gender	:	Male/Female
Type of Management of Schools	:	Government/Government Aided Self Finance Schools
Medium of Instruction	:	Tamil/English
Type of Family	:	Nuclear/Joint
Location of the School	:	Rural/Urban
Birth order	:	First born/Middle born/Last born

6. There is no significant difference in Confidence level - a dimension of Social Intelligence among Higher Secondary Students with regard to

Gender	:	Male/Female
Type of Management of Schools	:	Government/Government Aided /Self Finance Schools
Medium of Instruction	:	Tamil/English
Type of Family	:	Nuclear/Joint
Location of the School	:	Rural/Urban
Birth order	:	First born/Middle born/Last born

7. There is no significant difference in Sensitivity - a dimension of Social Intelligence among Higher Secondary Students with regard to

Gender	:	Male/Female
Type of Management of Schools	:	Government/ Government Aided/Self Finance Schools
Medium of Instruction	:	Tamil/English
Type of Family	:	Nuclear/Joint
Location of the School	:	Rural/Urban
Birth order	:	First born/Middle born/Last born

8. There is no significant difference in Recognition of Social Environment - a dimension of Social Intelligence among Higher Secondary Students with regard to

Gender	:	Male/Female
Type of Management of Schools	:	Government/ Government Aided /Self Finance Schools
Medium of Instruction	:	Tamil/English
Type of Family	:	Nuclear/Joint
Location of the School	:	Rural/Urban
Birth order	:	First born/Middle born/Last born

9. There is no significant difference in Tactfulness - a dimension of Social Intelligence among Higher Secondary Students with regard to

Gender	:	Male/Female
Type of Management of Schools	:	Government/Government Aided/Self Finance Schools
Medium of Instruction	:	Tamil/English
Type of Family	:	Nuclear/Joint
Location of the School	:	Rural/Urban
Birth order	:	First born/Middle born/Last born

10. There is no significant difference in Sense of Humour - a dimension of Social Intelligence among Higher Secondary Students with regard to

Gender	:	Male/Female
Type of Management of Schools	:	Government/Government Aided/Self Finance Schools
Medium of Instruction	:	Tamil/English

Type of Family	:	Nuclear/Joint
Location of the School	:	Rural/Urban
Birth order	:	First born/Middle born/Last born

11. There is no significant difference in Memory - a dimension of Social Intelligence among Higher Secondary Students with regard to

Gender	:	Male/Female
Type of Management of Schools	:	Government/ Government Aided /Self Finance Schools
Medium of Instruction	:	Tamil/English
Type of Family	:	Nuclear/Joint
Location of the School	:	Rural/Urban
Birth order	:	First born/Middle born/Last born

12. There is no significant difference in Subjective Happiness among Higher Secondary Students with regard to

Gender	:	Male/Female
Type of Management of Schools	:	Government/ Government Aided /Self Finance Schools
Medium of Instruction	:	Tamil/English
Type of Family	:	Nuclear/Joint
Location of the School	:	Rural/Urban
Birth order	:	First born/Middle born/Last born

13. There is no significant correlation between social Intelligence and Subjective Happiness of Higher Secondary Students.

METHOD OF STUDY

As the study intends to collect data pertaining to the Social Intelligence and Subjective Happiness, the normative method is employed to describe and interpret what exists at present. It involves some type of comparison or contrast and attempts to discover relationship between exiting non-manipulated variables.

TOOLS USED FOR THE PRESENT STUDY

1. Social Intelligence Scale constructed by Dr.N.K.Chadha and Ms.Usha Ganesan (2005).
2. Subjective Happiness Scale constructed by Sonja Lyumbomirsky (2010).

DESCRIPTION ADMINISTRATION AND SCORING PROCEDURE OF THE TOOLS USED IN THE PRESENT STUDY.

Social Intelligence Scale

Description

This scale (Appendix-I) consists of 54 items and 12 eminent persons constructed by Dr.N.K.Chadha and Ms.Usha Ganesan. This tool deals with 8 factors of Social Intelligence namely Patience, Co-operativeness, Confidence, Sensitivity, Recognition of Social Environment, Tactfulness, Sense of Humour and Memory.

TABLE.8.1: Showing Dimensions of Social Intelligence along with their Item Numbers

Social Intelligence Dimensions	Code Number	Item Numbers
Patience	A	4,8,15,16,20,27,33,36
Co-operativeness	B	1,5,9,14,17,21,25,26,28,31,32
Confidence Level	C	3,7,11,12,19,23,30,35
Sensitivity	D	2,6,10,13,18,22,24,29,34
Recognition of Social Environment	E	37,38,39
Tactfulness	F	40-46
Sense of Humour	G	47-54
Memory	H	55-66

Administration

The following instructions were given to the subjects before administrating the test. "There are some statements regarding the way in which we behave, feel and act. We want your first response. Please try to make your best possible answer honestly and sincerely. Read and understand each question properly and then put your mark on any cell against every statement on the answer sheet by making the sign of cross (x) please do not omit any question. In part I, read the following statements carefully and among the three responses given for each of them, pick up the one which seems to you to be the most likely way in which you would respond .You are to choose only one response from a ,b and c ,and make a cross (X) on the appropriate cell on the answer sheet .In part II, select the word that most accurately describes the mental state of the person making the statement. Cross out (X) the correct answer on the answer sheet .In part III, there are some statements regarding the way you behave and act. Each statement has a forced choice response of either 'Yes' or 'No'. Try and decide whether 'yes' or 'No' represents your usual way of behavior and acting. If yes, cross out (X) the cell below 'Yes' and if no, then cross out (X) the cell below 'No' . In part IV, list of incomplete jokes are given. Against them, there are three choices with which to complete the joke. You are to select and cross out (X) the choice you consider to be the most humorous. In part V list of eminent persons are given. You are supposed to identify them".

Scoring

In the case of 6 dimensions (Patience, Co-operativeness, Confidence Level and Sensitivity, Sense of Humour and Recognition of Social Environment) the subject was given a choice of three alternatives for each item and was asked to choose one.

In the case of the first four dimensions (Patience, Co-operativeness, Confidence Level and Sensitivity) scores of 1, 2, and 3 were given to three response alternatives. For e.g., in the Patience dimension a score of 3 would indicate a high degree of Patience ,a score of 1 a lack of Patience and a score of 2 would reveal moderate Patience.

TABLE.8.2: Showing the Scoring key for Patience

Items Nos.	**Response Alternatives**		
	A	B	c
4	1	3	2
8	2	3	1
15	1	2	3
16	1	3	2
20	1	2	3
27	3	1	2
33	3	2	1
36	2	3	1
		Scores Awarded	

In the other two dimensions (Sense of Humour and Recognition of social Environment) one of three alternatives given is the appropriate response. This response when given was allotted to scores of 1.

TABLE.8.3: Showing the Scoring key for Sense of Humour

Items Nos.	**Response Alternatives**		
	A	**B**	**C**
47	0	1	0
48	1	0	0
49	0	1	0
50	0	1	0
51	0	0	1
52	0	0	1
53	1	0	0
54	1	0	0
		Scores Awarded	

TABLE.8.4: Showing the Scoring key for Recognition of Social Environment

Items Nos.	**Response Alternatives**		
	A	B	C
37	1	0	0
38	1	0	0
39	0	1	0
		Scores Awarded	

In the case of the 'Tactfulness' dimension the responses were in the form of 'Yes' or 'NO' .The appropriate response was awarded a score of "1".

TABLE.8.5: Showing the Scoring key for Tactfulness

Items Nos.	**Response Alternatives**	
	Yes	**No**
40	0	1
41	0	1
42	0	1
43	1	0
44	0	1
45	1	0
46	1	0
		Scores Awarded

The last dimension that of Memory was scored '1'or '0'depending on whether or not the subject's response was 'right' or 'wrong'.

TABLE.8.6: Showing the Scoring key for Memory

Scoring of one (1) for following Correct responses
Indira Gandhi
Sachin Tendulkar
Ram Deo
C.V.Raman
Lata Mangeshkar
Prem Chand
Sarojini Naidu
Rabindranath Tagore
A.P.Abdul Kalam
Atal Behari Vajpai
Ashwarya Rai
Dr.Rajendra Prasad

Subjective Happiness Scale

Description

Sonja Lyubomirsky's Subjective Happiness Scale (2010) (Appendix-II) has been used in order to find out the level of subjective happiness of students .The standardized tool was in English .The scale consisted of four items. Out of which, three items are of positive items and one item is of negative item and it is based on seven point scale.

Administration

Students were asked to sit comfortably and to fill the tool. Even though there was no time limit to finish the questionnaire, students completed the task within 20 minutes. They were also told that their responses would be kept confidential and used strictly for the purpose of research only.

Scoring

Among the 4 items in the questionnaire one was negative and the rest were positive statements .The maximum possible score was 7.Four each statement, the students had seven options to mark their agreement or disagreement with statement

TABLE.8.7: Showing the nature of items in Subjective Happiness scale

S.No	Nature of item	Item Numbers	Score value
1	Positive	1, 2, 3	1 to 7
2	Negative	4	7 to 1

PILOT STUDY

Pilot study was effective in facilitating the final study. It helped the investigator in understanding the problem faced, while doing research work. The pilot study was conducted in October 2014 on 300 school students to establish reliability and validity of the research tools used in this study and to streamline the instruction to be given for each test.

ESTABLISHING RELIABILITY

The reliability of a test may be defined as the degree of consistency with which the test measures what it does measure .A test score is called reliable, when we have reasons for believing it to be stable and trust worthy **(S.P. Sakia 1963).**

The reliability of the tools used for present study was established as follows:

Social Intelligence Scale

In order to establish the reliability of the Social Intelligence scale, the split-half method was used. The reliability of the Social Intelligence scale was found to be .817.Hence Social Intelligence scale is considered as a valid tool.

Subjective Happiness

The test-retest reliability was found out for Subjective Happiness Scale. The computed value was 0.81 and hence the tool was highly reliable.

ESTABLISHING VALIDITY

Social Intelligence Scale

The Index of Validity which is the square root of reliability was found to be 0.9.Hence Social Intelligence scale selected for the study was considered to have high validity.

Subjective Happiness Scale

The square root of reliability, which is the index of validity, is found to be 0.9 .Hence the Subjective Happiness Scale was considered to have high validity.

MAIN STUDY

The validity tools were made use for the main study to collect the necessary data. The study was carried out in the month of December 2014 in 3 schools among of XI standard students in Thiruvannamalai District only.
The tools described below:

1. Social Intelligence Scale
2. Subjective Happiness Scale

Were used to collect the data for the main study, following the procedures mentioned for the administration of the test. The tests were administered on the samples of 300 XI standard students only.

TABLE.8.8: Showing the time Schedule of the tools Administered

S.No	Name of the Tool	Time Taken(Minutes)
1	Social Intelligence Scale	60
2	Subjective Happiness Scale	20

SAMPLE OF THE STUDY

Data was collected from the Higher Secondary students adopting stratified random sampling method. The total sample size was 300 drawn 3 schools were selected for the study belonging to different types of Management of Schools: Government, Government Aided and Self Finance schools. The details of schools visited and number of students tested for investigation is given below.

The details of the sample selected from different Types of Management of Schools in Thiruvannamalai District in given below.

TABLE.8.9: Showing the Details of the Sample Selected

S.No	Types of Management of Schools	Name and place of the school	Male	Female	Total
1	Government School	Shanmuga Industries Government Higher secondary school, Thiruvannamalai	50	50	100
2	Government Aided School	Danish Mission Higher Secondary school, Thiruvannamalai	50	50	100
3	Self Finance	Shishya Matric.Hr.Sec. School, Inamkariyandal village,Tiruvannamalai	50	50	100
		Total	**150**	**150**	**300**

STATISTICAL TECHNIQUES USED

a. Mean

Mean ($\bar{x}$) = $A + \frac{\sum fd}{\sum f} \times i$

Where,

A = Assumed mean

f = frequency

d = deviation from the assumed mean

i = Class interval

b. Standard Deviation

Standard Deviation, SD (σ) = $\sqrt{\frac{\sum fd^2}{N} - \left[\frac{\sum fd}{N}\right]^2} \times i$

Where,

f = Frequency

d = Deviation from the assumed mean

I = Class interval

N = Total frequency

c. 'T' TEST

To continue the significance of difference between means of various measures test is used: 't' ratio is calculated from the relation.

$$\text{t-ratio} = \frac{M_1 \sim M_2}{\sqrt{\frac{\sigma_1^2}{N_1} + \frac{\sigma_1^2}{N_2}}} = \frac{M_1 \sim M_2}{S \in D}$$

Where,

M_1, M_2 = Means of the groups

SED = S tandard Error Deviation

d. F-TEST

F- ratio = Variance between the group / Variance within the group Correlation term

$$C = \frac{\sum x_1 + \sum x_2 + \sum x_3}{N}$$

$$BSS = \left(\sum x_1\right)^2 / W_1 + \left(\sum x_2\right)^2 / W_2 + \left(\sum x_3\right)^2 W_3 - C$$

$$TSS = \sum x_1^2 + \sum x_2^2 + \sum x_3^2 - C$$

WSS = TSS - BSS

Where,

x_1, x_2, x_3, are score in different group

C = correction Term

TSS = Total Sum of Squares

BSS = Between Sum of Squares

WSS = Within Sum of Squares

e. Co-Efficient of Correlation (R)

$$r = \frac{N\sum x\sum y - \sum x\sum y}{\sqrt{\left(N\sum x^2 - \left(\sum x^2\right)\right)\left(N\sum y^2 - \left(\sum y\right)^2\right.}}$$

Where

N = Number of pairs of scores

x, y – Variables

CONLUSION

This chapter indicates the details regarding the design of the study, objectives, hypotheses, sample, pilot study, development of tools and techniques.

❒

9

Analysis and Interpretation

Research consists of systematic observation and description of the characteristic of properties for the purpose of discovering relationships, starts with the description of the measures of the variables and goes on to the higher levels of statistical analysis. The data collected will be carefully edited, systematically classified and tabulated, scientifically analyzed and interpreted and rationally concluded.

Thus, in the present study, the data were collected with regard to Social Intelligence. The data have been subjected to the following statistical analysis, namely percentile, descriptive, differential, correlation and association. The results of the statistical analysis have been summarized and tabulated.

For the investigator, analysis of collected data turns out to be a very important task. The information collected through the tools has been quantified as detailed in the following tables. For deciding the Social Intelligence of the higher secondary students with respect to Subjective Happiness, the following tables were prepared.

CARTEGORISATION OF THE SAMPLE BASED ON THE VARIABLES OF THE STUDY

Categories of the sample based on Social Intelligence

The sample has been classified on the basis of their Social Intelligence into their three categories (Low, Moderate and High), as indicated in the following table.

TABLE.9.1: Showing the level of Social Intelligence among Higher Secondary Students

Variable	Number of sample	Range	Level	Frequency	Percentage
Social Intelligence	300	96 and below	Low	78	26.0
		97 and 108	Moderate	131	43.7
		109 and above	High	91	30.3

INFERENCE

From the table, it is clear that the level of Social Intelligence among Higher Secondary Students is moderate in nature.

Hence hypothesis 1 stating that "The level of Social Intelligence of Higher Secondary Students is moderate in nature" is accepted.

Categories of the sample based on Subjective Happiness

The Higher Secondary Students has been classified on the basis of their Subjective Happiness into three categories (Low, Moderate and High), as indicated in the table given below.

TABLE.9.2: Showing the level of Subjective Happiness among the Higher Secondary Students

Variable	Number of sample	Range	Level	Frequency	Percentage
Subjective Happiness	300	16 and below	Low	94	31.3
		17 to 21	Moderate	126	42.0
		22 and above	High	80	26.7

INFERENCE

From the above table, it is found that the level of Subjective Happiness among the Higher Secondary Students is moderate in nature.

Hence hypotheses - 2 stating that "The level of Subjective Happiness of Higher Secondary Students is moderate in nature" is accepted.

INFLUENCE OF GENDER ON SOCIAL INTELLIGECE

The scores related to Social Intelligence of Male and Female Higher Secondary Students have been computed and details are furnished in the following table.

TABLE.9.3: Showing the Significant Difference between the mean Scores of Social Intelligence with Respect to Gender

Variable	Gender	N	Mean	S.D	Critical Ratio	L.S
Social Intelligence	Males	150	100.32	11.880	3.321	0.01
	Females	150	104.24	8.241		

INFERENCE

From the table, it is clear that the obtained C. R value (3.321) is greater than the table value (2.58) at 0.01 level. Therefore there is significant difference between the mean scores of Social Intelligence among Higher Secondary Students with regard to Gender.

Moreover, Female students have higher Social Intelligence than their counterparts.

Hence the hypothesis – 3 (a) stating that "There is no significant difference between the mean scores of Social Intelligence among Higher Secondary Students with regard to Gender" is rejected.

INFLUENCE OF TYPE OF MANAGEMENT OF SCHOOLS ON SOCIAL INTELLIGENCE

The scores related to Social Intelligence of Government, Governmen Aided and Self Finance Higher Secondary Students have been computed and details are furnished in the following table.

TABLE.9.4: ANOVA Showing the Significant Difference between the mean Scores of Social Intelligence with Respect to Type of Management of Schools

Variable		Sum of Squares	df	Mean Squares	'F' Value	L.S
Social Intelligence	Between Groups	937.580	2	468.790	4.439	0.05
	Within Groups	31362.900	297	105.599		
	Total	**35980.990**	**299**			

INFERENCE

From the table, it is clear that the obtained 'F' value (4.439) is greater than the table value (3.03)at 0.05 level. Therefore there is significant difference between the mean scores of Social Intelligence among Higher Secondary Students with regard to Type of Management of Schools.So, further analysis has been done between the groups.

TABLE.9.5: Showing the Mean, S.D and C.R Value for Social Intelligence of Higher Secondary Students based on Type of Management of Schools

Variable	Type of Management of Schools	F	Mean	Std Deviation	C.R Value	L.S
Social Intelligence	Government Vs Government Aided	100	104.43	7.865	3.138	0.01
		100	100.10	11.338		
	Government Aided Vs Self Finance	100	100.10	11.338	1.384	N.S
		100	102.31	11.242		
	Self Finance Vs Government	100	102.31	11.242	1.545	N.S
		100	104.43	7.865		

INFERENCE

From the above table, the following inferences have been made.

n the first case, the calculated value (3.138) is greater than table value (2.58) at 0.01 level of significance, showing that there is significant difference between students studying in Government and Government Aided Higher Secondary schools with regard to Social Intelligence.

In the second case, the calculated value (1.384) is lesser than the table value (1.96) at 0.05 level of significance, showing that there is no significant difference between students studying in Government Aided and self finance Higher Secondary schools with regard to Social Intelligence.

In the third case, the calculated value (1.545) is lesser than the expected table value (1.96) at 0.05 level of significance, showing that there is no significant difference between students studying in Self finance and Government Higher Secondary schools with regard to Social Intelligence.

Moreover, Government school students have significantly Higher Social Intelligence than the students studying in Government Aided and Self Finance schools.

Hence the hypothesis – 3(b) stating that " There is no significant difference between the mean scores of Social Intelligence among Higher Secondary Students with regard to Type of Management of Schools" is partially verified.

INFLUENCE OF MEDIUM OF INSTRUCTION ON SOCIAL INTELLIGENCE

The scores related to Social Intelligence of Tamil and English medium of Higher Secondary Students have been computed and details are furnished in the following table.

TABLE.9.6: Showing the Significant Difference between the mean Scores of Social Intelligence with Respect to Medium of Instruction

Variable	Medium of Instruction	N	Mean	S.D	Critical Ratio	L.S
Social Intelligence	Tamil	221	102.52	9.227	.669	N.S
	English	79	101.61	13.166		

INFERENCE

From the table, it is clear that the obtained C. R value (.669) is lower than the table value (1.96) at 0.05 level. Therefore there is no significant difference between the mean scores of Social Intelligence among Higher Secondary Students with regard to Medium of Instruction.

Hence the hypothesis – 3 (c) stating that " There is no significant difference between the mean scores of Social Intelligence among Higher Secondary Students with regard to Medium of Instruction" is accepted.

INFLUENCE OF TYPE OF FAMILY ON SOCIAL INTELLIGENCE

The scores related to Social Intelligence of Higher Secondary Students hailing from Nuclear and Joint families have been computed and details are furnished in the following table.

TABLE.9.7: Showing the Significant Difference between the mean Scores of Social Intelligence with Respect to Type of Family

Variable	Type of Family	N	Mean	S.D	Critical Ratio	L.S
Social Intelligence	Nuclear	160	102.33	9.902	.091	N.S
	Joint	140	102.33	10.964		

INFERENCE

From the table, it is clear that the obtained C. R value (.091) is lower than the table value(1.96) at 0.05 level. Therefore there is no significant difference between the mean scores of Social Intelligence among Higher Secondary Students with regard to Type of Family.

Hence the hypothesis – 3 (d) stating that "There is no significant difference between the mean scores of Social Intelligence among Higher Secondary Students with regard to Type of Family" is accepted.

INFLUENCE OF LOCATION OF THE SCHOOL ON SOCIAL INTELLIGENCE

The scores related to Social Intelligence of Rural and Urban Higher Secondary Students have been computed and details are furnished in the following table.

TABLE.9.8: Showing the Significant Difference between the mean Scores of Social Intelligence with Respect to Location of the School

Variable	Location of the School	N	Mean	S.D	Critical Ratio	L.S
Social Intelligence	Rural	100	102.31	11.242	.035	N.S
	Urban	200	102.27	9.972		

INFERENCE

From the table, it is clear that the obtained C. R value (0.35) is lower than the table value (1.96) at 0.05 level. Therefore there is no significant difference between the mean scores of Social Intelligence among Higher Secondary Students regards to Location of the School.

Hence the hypothesis – 3 (e) stating that "There is no significant difference between the mean scores of Social Intelligence among Higher Secondary Students with regard to Location of the School" is accepted.

INFLUENCE OF BIRTH ORDER ON SOCIAL INTELLIGENCE

The scores related to Social Intelligence of First born, Middle born and Last born Higher Secondary Students have been computed and details are furnished in the following table.

TABLE.9.9: ANOVA Showing the Significant Difference between the mean Scores of Social Intelligence with Respect to Birth Order

Variable		Sum of Squares	df	Mean Squares	'F' Value	L.S
Social Intelligence	Between Groups	937.771	2	2.644	4.440	0.05
	Within Groups	35975.710	297	104.277		
	Total	**35980.997**	**299**			

INFERENCE

From the table, it is clear that the obtained 'F' value (4.440) is greater than the table value (3.03)at 0.05 level. Therefore there is significant difference between the mean scores of Social Intelligence among Higher Secondary Students with regard to Birth Order. So, further analysisn has been done between the groups.

TABLE .9.10: Showing the Mean, S.D and C.R value for Social Intelligence of Higher Secondary Students based on Birth Order

Variable	Birth order	N	Mean	Std Deviation	C.R Value	L.S
Social Intelligence	First born Vs Middle born	101	101.52	11.199	2.200	0.05
		111	104.50	8.440		
	Middle born Vs Last born	111	104.50	8.440	2.984	0.01
		88	100.34	11.237		
	Last born Vs First born	88	100.34	11.237	.724	N.S
		101	101.52	11.199		

INFERENCE

From the above table, the following inferences have been made.

In the first case, the calculated value (2.200) is higher than table value (1.96) at 0.05 level of significance, showing that there is significant difference between First born and Middle born students with regard to Social Intelligence.

In the second case, the calculated value (2.984) is higher than the table value (1.96) at 0.01 level of significance, showing that there is significant difference between Middle born and last born students with regard to Social Intelligence.

In the third case, the calculated value (.724) is lesser than the expected table value (2.58) at 0.05 level of significance, showing that there is no significant difference between Last born and First born students and with regard to Social Intelligence .

Moreover, Middle born students have exhibited significantly higher Social Intelligence than First born and last born students.

Hence the hypothesis – 3(f) stating that " There is no significant difference between the mean scores of Social Intelligence among Higher Secondary Students with regard to Birth Order" is partially verified.

INFLUENCE OF GENDER ON PATIENCE-A DIMENSION OF SOCIAL INTELLIGENCE

The scores related to Patience-a dimension of Social Intelligence of Male and Female Higher Secondary Students have been computed and details are furnished in the following table.

TABLE.9.11: Showing the Significant Difference between the mean Scores of Patience-a Dimension of Social Intelligence with Respect to Gender

Variable	Gender	N	Mean	S.D	Critical Ratio	L.S
Patience	Males	150	18.33	2.953	3.585	0.01
	Females	150	19.55	2.909		

INFERENCE

From the table, it is clear that the obtained C. R value (3.585) is greater than the table value(2.58) at 0.01 at level. Therefore there is significant difference between the mean scores of Patience-a dimension of social Intelligence among Higher Secondary Students with regard to Gender.

Female students have significantly higher Patience-a dimension of Social Intelligence than their counter parts.

Hence the hypothesis –4 (a) stating that "There is no significant difference between the mean scores of Patience-a dimension of Social Intelligence among Higher Secondary Students with regard to Gender" is rejected.

INFLUENCE OF TYPE OF MANAGEMENT ON PATIENCE A DIMENSION OF SOCIAL INTELLIGENCE

The scores related to Patience-a dimension of Social Intelligence of Government, Government- Aided and Self Finance Higher Secondary Students have been computed and details are furnished in the following table.

TABLE.9.12: ANOVA Showing the Significant Difference between the mean Scores of Patience-a Dimension of Social Intelligence with Respect to Type of Management of Schools.

Variable		Sum of Squares	df	Mean Squares	'F' Value	L.S
Patience	Between Groups	24.240	2	112.120	13.610	0.01
	Within Groups	2446.680	297	8.238		
	Total	**2670.920**	**299**			

INFERENCE

From the table, it is clear that the obtained 'F' value (13.610) is greater than the table value (4.68) at 0.01 level. Therefore there is significant difference between the mean scores of Patience-a dimension of Social Intelligence among Higher Secondary Students with regard to Type of Management of Schools. So, further analysis has been done between the groups.

TABLE.9.13: Showing the Mean, S.D and C.R value for Patience- a Dimension of Social Intelligence of Higher Secondary Students based on Type of Management of Schools

Variable	Type of Management of Schools	F	Mean	Std Deviation	C.R Value	L.O.S
Patience	Government Vs Government Aided	100	20.16	2.489	4.423	0.01
		100	18.40	3.104		
	Government Aided Vs Self Finance	100	18.40	3.104	0.325	N.S
		100	18.26	2.980		
	Self Finance Vs Government	100	18.26	2.980	4.893	0.01
		100	20.16	2.489		

INFERENCE

From the above table, following inferences have been made.

In the first case, the calculated value (4.423) is greater than table value (2.58) at 0.01 level of significance, showing that there is significant difference between students studying in Government and Government Aided Higher Secondary schools with regard to Patience-a dimension of Social Intelligence.

In the second case, the calculated value (0.325) is lower than the table value (1.96) at 0.05 level of significance, showing that there is no significant difference between students studying in Government Aided and Self Finance Higher Secondary schools with regard to Patience-a dimension of Social Intelligence.

In the third case, the calculated value (4.893) is greater than the expected table value (2.58) at 0.01 level of significance, showing that there is significant difference between students studying in Self Finance and Government Higher Secondary schools with regard to Patience-a dimension of Social Intelligence.

Moreover, Government school students have significantly higher Patience-a dimension of Social Intelligence than Government Aided and Self Finance school students.

Hence the hypothesis – 4 (b) stating that "There is no significant difference between the mean scores of Patience-a dimension of Social Intelligence among Higher Secondary Students with regard to Type of Management of Schools" is partially verified.

INFLUENCE OF MEDIUM OF INSTRUCTION ON PATIENCE A-DIMENSION OF SOCIAL INTELLIGENCE

The scores related to Patience-a dimension of Social Intelligence of Tamil and English medium Higher Secondary Students have been computed and details are furnished in the following table.

TABLE. 4.14: Showing the Significant Difference between the mean Scores of Patience-a Dimension of Social Intelligence with Respect to Medium of Instruction

Variable	Medium of Instruction	N	Mean	S.D	Critical Ratio	L.S
Patience	Tamil	221	19.17	2.818	2.219	0.05
	English	79	18.30	3.360		

INFERENCE

From the table, it is clear that the obtained C.R value (2.219) is greater than the table value (1.96) at 0.05 level. Therefore there is significant difference between the mean scores of Patience-a dimension of Social Intelligence among Higher Secondary Students with regard to Medium of Instruction.

Tamil medium students have significantly higher Patience-a dimension of Social Intelligence than their English medium students.

Hence the hypothesis – 4 (c) stating that "There is no significant difference between the mean scores of Patience-a dimension of Social Intelligence among Higher Secondary Students with regard to Medium of Instruction" is rejected.

INFLUENCE OF TYPE OF FAMILY ON PATIENCE -A DIMENSION OF SOCIAL INTELLIGENCE

The scores related to Patience-a dimension of Social Intelligence of Higher Secondary Students hailing from Nuclear and Joint families have been computed and details are furnished in the following table.

TABLE.9.15: Showing the Significant Difference between the mean Scores of Patience- a Dimension of Social Intelligence with Respect to Type of Family

Variable	Type of Family	N	Mean	S.D	Critical Ratio	L.S
Patience	Nuclear	140	18.79	3.072	0.836	N.S
	Joint	160	19.08	2.917		

INFERENCE

From the table, it is clear that the obtained C.R value (0.836) is lower than the table value (1.96) at 0.05 level. Therefore there is no significant difference between the mean scores of Patience-a dimension of Social Intelligence among Higher Secondary Students with regard to Type of family.

Hence the hypothesis – 4 (d) stating that "There is no significant difference between the mean scores of Patience-a dimension of Social Intelligence among Higher Secondary Students with regard to Type of family" is accepted.

INFLUENCE OF LOCATION OF THE SCHOOL ON PATIENCE-A DIMENSION OF SOCIAL INTELLIGENCE

The scores related to Patience-a dimension of Social Intelligence of Rural and Urban Higher Secondary Students have been computed and details are furnished in the following table.

TABLE .916: Showing the Significant Difference between the mean Scores of Patience- a Dimension of Social Intelligence with Respect to Location of the School

Variable	Location of the School	N	Mean	S.D	Critical Ratio	L.S
Patience	Rural	100	18.26	2.980	2.819	0.01
	Urban	200	19.28	2.942		

INFERENCE

From the table, it is clear that the obtained C.R value (2.819) is greater than the table value (2.58) at 0.01 level. Therefore there is significant difference between the mean scores of Patience-a dimension of Social Intelligence among Higher Secondary Students with regard to Location of the School.

Moreover, Urban students have significantly higher Patience-a dimension of Social Intelligence than Rural students.

Hence the hypothesis – 4 (e) stating that "There is no significant difference between the mean scores of Patience-a dimension of Social Intelligence among Higher Secondary Students with regard to Location of the School" is rejected.

INFLUENCE OF BIRTH ORDER ON PATIENCE-A DIMENSION OF SOCIAL INTELLIGENCE

The scores related to Patience-a dimension of Social Intelligence of First born, Middle born and Last born Higher Secondary Students have been computed and details are furnished in the following table.

TABLE. 9.17: ANOVA Showing the Significant Difference between the mean Scores of Patience-a Dimension of Social Intelligence with Respect to Birth Order

Variable		Sum of Squares	df	Mean Squares	'F' Value	L.S
Patience	Between Groups	17.943	2	8.971	1.004	N. S
	Within Groups	2652.977	297	8.933		
	Total	**2670.920**	**299**			

INFERENCE

From the table, it is clear that the obtained 'F' value (1.004) is lower than the table value (1.96) at 0.05 level. Therefore there is no significant difference between the mean scores of Patience-a dimension of Social Intelligence among Higher Secondary Students with regard to Birth Order.

Hence the hypothesis – 4 (f) stating that "There is no significant difference between the mean scores of Patience-a dimension of Social Intelligence among Higher Secondary Students with regard to Birth Order" is accepted.

INFLUENCE OF GENDER ON CO-OPERATIVENESS -A DIMENSION OF SOCIAL INTELLIGENCE

The scores related to Co-operativeness-a dimension of Social Intelligence of Male and Female Higher Secondary Students have been computed and details are furnished in the following table.

TABLE.9.18: Showing the Significant Difference between the mean Scores of Co-Operativeness-a Dimension of Social Intelligence with Respect to Gender

Variable	Gender	N	Mean	S.D	Critical Ratio	L.S
Cooperativeness	Males	150	24.65	4.062	2.574	0.05
	Females	150	25.77	3.400		

INFERENCE

From the table, it is clear that the obtained C.R value (2.574) is greater than the table value (2.58) at 0.05 level. Therefore there is significant difference between the mean scores of Co-operativeness-a dimension Social Intelligence among Higher Secondary Students with regard to Gender.

Moreover, girls have significantly higher Co-operativeness-a dimension of Social Intelligence than their counter parts.

Hence the hypothesis – 5 (a) stating that "There is no significant difference between the mean scores of Co-operativeness-a dimension of Social Intelligence among Higher Secondary Students with regard to Gender" is rejected.

INFLUENCE OF TYPE OF MANAGEMENT ON CO-OPERATIVENESS -A DIMENSION OF SOCIAL INTELLIGENCE

The scores related to Co-operativeness-a dimension of Social Intelligence of Government, Government Aided and Self Finance Higher Secondary Students have been computed and details are furnished in the following table.

TABLE.9.19: ANOVA Showing the Significant Difference between the mean Scores of Co-Operativeness-a Dimension of Social Intelligence with Respect to Type of Management of Schools

Variable		Sum of Squares	df	Mean Squares	'F' Value	L.S
Cooperativeness	Between Groups	108.620	2	54.310	3.873	0.05
	Within Groups	4165.150	297	14.024		
	Total	**4273.770**	**299**			

INFERENCE

From the table, it is clear that the obtained 'F' value (3.873) is greater than the table value (3.03) at 0.05 level. Therefore there is significant difference between the mean scores of Co-operativeness-a dimension of Social Intelligence among Higher Secondary Students with regard to Type of Management of Schools. So, further analysis has been done between the groups.

TABLE.9.20: Showing the Mean, S.D and C.R value for Co-operativeness -a Dimension of Social Intelligence of Higher Secondary Students based on Type of Management of Schools

Variable	Type of Management of Schools	F	Mean	Std Deviation	C.R Value	L.S
Cooperativeness	Government Vs Government Aided	100	26.06	2.933	2.417	0.05
		100	24.82	4.210		
	Government Aided Vs Self Finance	100	24.82	4.210	.121	NS
		100	24.75	3.968		
	Self Finance Vs Government		24.75	3.968	2.655	0.01
		100	26.06	2.933		

INFERENCE

From the above table, following inferences have been made.

In the first case, the calculated value (2.417) is greater than table value (1.96) at 0.05 level of significance, showing that there is significant difference between students studying in Government and Government Aided Higher Secondary schools with regard to Co-operativeness -a dimension of Social Intelligence.

In the second case, the calculated value (.121) is lower than the table value (1.96) at 0.05 level of significance, showing that there is no significant difference between students studying in Government Aided and Self Finance Higher Secondary schools with regard to Co-operativeness -a dimension of Social Intelligence.

In the third case, the calculated value (2.655) is greater than the expected table value (2.58) at 0.01 level of significance, showing that there is significant difference between students studying in Self Finance and Government Higher Secondary schools with regard to Co-operativeness -a dimension of Social Intelligence.

Moreover, Government school students have significantly higher Co-operativeness -a dimension of Social Intelligence than in Government Aided and Self Finance school students.

Hence the hypothesis – 5 (b) stating that "There is no significant difference between the mean scores of Co-operativeness-a dimension of Social Intelligence among Higher Secondary Students with regard to Type of Management of Schools" is partially verified.

INFLUENCE OF MEDIUM OF INSTRUCTION ON CO-OPERATIVENESS- A DIMENSION OF SOCIAL INTELLIGENCE

The scores related to Co-operativeness-a dimension of Social Intelligence of Tamil and English medium Higher Secondary Students have been computed and details are furnished in the following table.

TABLE.9.21: Showing the Significant Difference between the mean Scores of Co-Operativeness-a Dimension of Social Intelligence with Respect to Medium of Instruction

Variable	Medium of Instruction	N	Mean	S.D	Critical Ratio	L.S
Cooperativeness	Tamil	221	25.38	3.511	1.305	N.S
	English	79	24.73	4.440		

INFERENCE

From the table, it is clear that the obtained C.R value (1.305) is lower than the table value (1.96) at 0.05 level. Therefore there is no significant difference between the mean scores of Co- operativeness-a dimension of Social Intelligence among Higher Secondary Students with regard to Medium of Instruction.

Hence the hypothesis – 5 (c) stating that "There is no significant difference between the mean scores of Co-operativeness-a dimension of Social Intelligence among Higher Secondary Students with regard to Medium of Instruction" is accepted.

INFLUENCE OF TYPE OF FAMILY ON CO-OPERATIVENESS – A DIMENSION OF SOCIAL INTELLIGENCE

The scores related to Co-operativeness-a dimension of Social Intelligence of Higher Secondary Students hailing from Nuclear and Joint families have been computed and details are furnished in the following table.

TABLE.9.22: Showing the Significant Difference between the mean Scores of Co-Operativeness-a Dimension of Social Intelligence with Respect to Type of Family

Variable	Type of Family	N	Mean	S.D	Critical Ratio	L.S
Cooperativeness	Nuclear	160	25.43	3.753	1.053	N.S
	Joint	140	24.96	3.811		

INFERENCE

From the table, it is clear that the obtained C.R value (1.053) is lower than the table value (1.96) at 0.05 level. Therefore there is no significant difference between the mean scores of Co- operativeness-a dimension of Social Intelligence among Higher Secondary Students with regard to Type of Family.

Hence the hypothesis–5 (d) stating that "There is no significant difference between the mean scores of Co- operativeness-a dimension of Social Intelligence among Higher Secondary Students with regard to Type of Family" is accepted.

INFLUENCE OF LOCATION OF THE SCHOOL ON CO-OPERATIVENESS –A DIMENSION OF SOCIAL INTELLIGENCE

The scores related to Co- operativeness-a dimension of Social Intelligence of Rural and Urban Higher secondary Students have been computed and details are furnished in the following table.

TABLE.9.23: Showing the Significant Difference between the mean Scores of Co-Operativeness-a Dimension of Social Intelligence with Respect to Location of the School

Variable	Location of the School	N	Mean	S.D	Critical Ratio	L.S
Cooperativeness	Rural	100	24.75	3.968	1.493	N.S
	Urban	200	25.44	3.672		

INFERENCE

From the table, it is clear that the obtained C. R value (1.493) is lower than the table value (1.96) at 0.05 level. Therefore there is no significant difference between the mean scores of Co-operativeness-a dimension of Social Intelligence among Higher Secondary Students with regard to Location of the School .

Hence the hypothesis – 5 (e) stating that "There is no significant difference between the mean scores of Co-operativeness-a dimension of Social Intelligence among Higher Secondary Students with regard to Location of the School" is accepted.

INFLUENCE OF BIRTH ORDER ON COOPERATIVENESS - A DIMENSION OF SOCIAL INTELLIGENCE

The scores related to Co- operativeness-a dimension of Social Intelligence of First born, Middle born and Last born Higher Secondary Students have been computed and details are furnished in the following table.

TABLE.9.24: ANOVA Showing the Significant Difference between the mean Scores of Co- Operativeness-a Dimension of Social Intelligence with Respect to Birth Order

Variable		Sum of Squares	df	Mean Squares	'F' Value	L.S
Cooperativeness	Between Groups	34.625	2	17.313	1.213	N. S
	Within Groups	4239.145	297	14.273		
	Total	**4273.770**	**299**			

INFERENCE

From the table, it is clear that the obtained 'F' value (1.213) is lower than the table value (3.03) at 0.05 level. Therefore there is no significant difference between the mean scores of Social Intelligence among Higher Secondary Students with regard to Birth Order.

Hence the hypothesis – 5 (f) stating that "There is no significant differnce between the mean scores of Co-operativeness-a dimension of Social Intelligence among Higher Secondary Students with regard to Birth order" is accepted.

INFLUENCE OF GENDER ON CONFIDENCE LEVEL - A DIMENSION OF SOCIAL INTELLIGENCE

The scores related to Confidence Level-a dimension of Social Intelligence of Males and Females of Higher Secondary Students have been computed and details are furnished in the following table.

TABLE. 9.25: Showing the Significant Difference between the mean Scores of Confidence Level -a Dimension of Social Intelligence with Respect to Gender

Variable	Gender	N	Mean	S.D	Critical Ratio	L.S
Confidence Level	Males	150	18.35	3.468	3.244	0.01
	Females	150	19.45	2.284		

INFERENCE

From the table, it is clear that the obtained C. R value (3.244) is greater than the table value (2.58) at 0.01 level. Therefore there is significant difference between the mean scores of Confidence Level-a dimension of Social Intelligence among Higher Secondary Students with regard to Gender.

Moreover, Female students have significantly higher Confidence Level -a dimension of Social Intelligence than their counter parts.

Hence the hypothesis–6 (a) stating that "There is no significant difference between the mean scores of Confidence Level-a dimension of Social Intelligence among Higher Secondary Students with regard to Gender" is rejected.

INFLUENCE OF TYPE OF MANAGEMENT OF SCHOOLS ON CONFIDENCE LEVEL-A DIMENSION OF SOCIAL INTELLIGENCE

The scores related to Confidence Level-a dimension of Social Intelligence of Government, Government-Aided and Self Finance Higher Secondary Students have been computed and details are furnished in the following table.

TABLE.9.26: ANOVA Showing the Significant Difference between the mean Scores of Confidence Level -a Dimension of Social Intelligence with Respect to Type of Management of Schools.

Variable		Sum of Squares	df	Mean Squares	'F' Value	L.S
Confidence Level	Between Groups	125.627	2	62.813	7.360	0.01
	Within Groups	2534.570	297	8.534		
	Total	**2660.197**	**299**			

INFERENCE

From the table, it is clear that the obtained 'F' value (7.360) is greater than the table value (4.68) at 0.01 level. Therefore there is significant difference between the mean scores of Confidence Level-a dimension of Social Intelligence among Higher Secondary Students with regard to Type of Management of Schools. So, further analysis has been done between the groups.

TABLE.9.27: Showing the Mean, S.D and C.R value for Confidence Level -a Dimension of -a Dimension Social Intelligence of Higher Secondary Students based on Type of Management of Schools

Variable	Type of Management of Schools.	F	Mean	Std Deviation	C.R Value	L.S
Confidence Level	Government VsGovernment Aided	100	19.73	2.309	2.339	0.05
		100	18.83	3.078		
	Government Aided Vs Self Finance	100	18.83	3.078	1.510	N.S
		100	18.15	3.286		
	Self Finance Vs Government	100	18.15	3.286	3.935	0.01
		100	19.73	2.309		

INFERENCE

From the above table, following inferences have been made.

In the first case, the calculated value (2.339) is greater than table value (1.96) at 0.05 level of significance, showing that there is significant difference between students studying in Government and Government Aided Higher Secondary schools with regard to Confidence Level-a dimension of Social Intelligence .

In the second case, the calculated value (1.510) is lesser than the table value (1.96) at 0.05 level of significance, showing that there is no significant difference between students studying in Government Aided and Self Finance Higher Secondary schools with regard to Confidence Level-a dimension of Social Intelligence .

In the third case, the calculated value (3.935) is greater than the expected table value (2.56) at 0.01 level of significance, showing that there is significant difference between students studying in Self Finance and Government Higher Secondary schools with regard to Confidence-a dimension of Social Intelligence

Moreover, Government school students have significantly higher Confidence Level than students studying in Government Aided and Self Finance schools.

Hence the hypothesis– 6 (b) stating that "There is no significant difference between the mean scores of Confidence-a dimension of -a dimension Social Intelligence among Higher Secondary Students with regard to Type of Management of Schools " is partially verified.

INFLUENCE OF MEDIUM OF INSTRUCTION ON CONFIDENCE LEVEL-A DIMENSION OF SOCIAL INTELLIGENCE

The scores related to Confidence Level-a dimension of Social Intelligence of Tamil and English medium Higher Secondary Students have been computed and details are furnished in the following table.

TABLE.9.28: Showing the Significant Difference between the mean Scores of Confidence-a Dimension of Social Intelligence with Respect to Medium of Instruction

Variable	Medium of Instruction	N	Mean	S.D	Critical Ratio	L.S
Confidence Level	Tamil	221	19.12	2.777	2.093	0.05
	English	79	18.30	3.443		

INFERENCE

From the table, it is clear that the obtained C. R value (2.093) is greater than the table value (1.96) at 0.05 level. Therefore there is significant difference between the mean scores of Confidence-a dimension of Social Intelligence among Higher Secondary Students with regard to Medium of Instruction.

Moreover, Tamil medium students have significantly higher Confidence Level than their counter parts.

Hence the hypothesis–6 (c) stating that "There is no significant difference between the mean scores of Confidence-a dimension of Social Intelligence among Higher Secondary Students with regard to Medium of Instruction" is rejected.

INFLUENCE OF TYPE OF FAMILY ON CONFIDENCE LEVEL -A DIMENSION OF SOCIAL INTELLIGENCE

The scores related to Confidence Level -a dimension of Social Intelligence of Higher Secondary Students hailing from Nuclear and Joint families have been computed and details are furnished in the following table.

TABLE.9.29: Showing the Significant Difference between the mean Scores of Confidence Level -a Dimension of Social Intelligence with Respect to Type of Family

Variable	Type of Family	N	Mean	S.D	Critical Ratio	L.S
Confidence Level	Nuclear	160	18.98	2.728	0.483	N.S
	Joint	140	18.81	3.258		

INFERENCE

From the table, it is clear that the obtained C. R value (0.483) is lower than the table value (1.96) at 0.05 level. Therefore there is no significant difference between the mean scores of Confidence Level -a dimension of

Social Intelligence among Higher Secondary Students with regard to Type of Family.

Hence the hypothesis – 6 (d) stating that "There is no significant difference between the mean scores of Confidence Level-a dimension of Social Intelligence among Higher Secondary Students with regard to Type of Family" is accepted.

INFLUENCE OF LOCATION OF THE SCHOOL ON CONFIDENCE LEVEL -A DIMENSION OF SOCIAL INTELLIGENCE

The scores related to Confidence Level -a dimension of Social Intelligence of Rural and Urban Higher Secondary Students have been computed and details are furnished in the following table.

TABLE.9.30: Showing the Significant Difference between the mean Scores of Confidence Level -a Dimension of Social Intelligence with Respect to Location of the School

Variable	Location of the School	N	Mean	S.D	Critical Ratio	L.S
Confidence Level	Rural	100	18.15	3.286	3.139	0.01
	Urban	200	19.28	2.751		

INFERENCE

From the table, it is clear that the obtained C. R value (3.139) is greater than the table value (2.58) at 0.01 level. Therefore there is significant difference between the mean scores of Confidence Level-a dimension of Social intelligence among Higher Secondary Students with regard to Location of the School .

Moreover, urban students have significantly higher confidence Level -a dimension of Social Intelligence than rural students.

Hence the hypothesis – 6 (e) stating that "There is no significant difference between the mean scores of Confidence Level-a dimension of Social Intelligence among Higher Secondary Students with regard to Location of the School" is rejected.

INFLUENCE OF BIRTH ORDER ON CONFIDENCE LEVEL - A DIMENSION OF SOCIAL INTELLIGENCE

The scores related to Confidence Level -a dimension of Social Intelligence of First born ,Middle born and Last born Higher Secondary Students have been computed and details are furnished in the following table.

TABLE.9.31: ANOVA Showing the Significant Difference between the mean Scores of Confidence Level -a Dimension of Social Intelligence with Respect to Birth Order

Variable		Sum of Squares	df	Mean Squares	'F' Value	L.S
Confidence Level	Between Groups	37.660	2	18.830	2.132	N. S
	Within Groups	2622.537	297	8.830		
	Total	**2660.197**	**299**			

INFERENCE

From the table, it is clear that the obtained 'F' value (2.132) is lower than the table value (3.03) at 0.05 level. Therefore there is no significant difference between the mean scores of Confidence Level -a dimension of Social Intelligence among Higher Secondary Students with regard to Birth Order.

Hence the hypothesis –6(f) stating that "There is no significant difference between the mean scores of Confidence Level-a dimension of Social Intelligence among Higher Secondary Students with regard to Birth Order" is accepted.

INFLUENCE OF GENDER ON SENSITIVITY-A DIMENSION OF SOCIAL INTELLIGENCE

The scores related to Sensitivity-a dimension of Social Intelligence of Male and Female Higher Secondary Students have been computed and details are furnished in the following table.

TABLE.9.32: Showing the Significant Difference between the mean Scores of Sensitivity -a Dimension of Social Intelligence with Respect to Gender

Variable	Gender	N	Mean	S.D	Critical Ratio	L.S
Sensitivity	Males	150	20.10	3.417	2.880	0.01
	Females	150	21.10	2.532		

INFERENCE

From the table, it is clear that the obtained C.R value (2.880) is greater than the table value (2.58) at 0.01 level. Therefore there is significant difference between the mean scores of Sensitivity -a dimension of Social Intelligence among Higher Secondary Students with regard to Gender.

Girls have significantly higher Sensitivity -a dimension of Social Intelligence than their counter parts.

Hence the hypothesis –7 (a) stating that " There is no significant difference between the mean scores of Sensitivity-a dimension of social Intelligence among Higher Secondary Students with regard to Gender" is rejected.

INFLUENCE OF TYPE OF MANAGEMENT OF SCHOOLS ON SENSITIVITY-A DIMENSION OF SOCIAL INTELLIGENCE

The scores related to Sensitivity -a dimension of Social Intelligence of Government, Government Aided and Self Finance Higher Secondary Students have been computed and details are furnished in the following table.

TABLE.9.33: ANOVA Showing the Significant Difference between the mean Scores of Sensitivity -a Dimension of Social Intelligence with Respect to Type of Management of Schools.

Variable		Sum of Squares	df	Mean Squares	'F' Value	L.S
Sensitivity	Between Groups	158.540	2	79.270	9.015	0.01
	Within Groups	2611.460	297	8.793		
	Total	**2770.000**	**299**			

INFERENCE

From the table, it is clear that the obtained 'F' value (9.015) is greater than the table value (4.68) at 0.01 level. Therefore there is significant difference between the mean scores of Sensitivity-a dimension of Social Intelligence among Higher Secondary Students with regard to Type of Management of Schools. So, further analysis has been done between the groups.

TABLE.9.34: Showing the Mean, S.D and C.R value for Sensitivity -a Dimension of Social Intelligence of Higher Secondary Students based on Type of Management of Schools

Variable	Type of Management of Schools	F	Mean	Std Deviation	C.R Value	L.S
Sensitivity	Government Vs Government Aided	100	21.57	2.119	2.740	0.01
		100	20.41	3.666		
	Government Aided Vs Self Finance SF	100	20.41	3.666	1.261	N.S
		100	19.82	2.907		
	Self Finance Vs Government	100	19.82	2.907	4.864	0.01
		100	21.57	2.119		

INFERENCE

From the above table, following inferences have been made.

In the first case, the calculated value (2.740) is greater than table value (2.58) at 0.01 level of significance, showing that there is significant difference between students studying in Government and Government Aided Higher Secondary schools with regard to Sensitivity-a dimension of Social Intelligence.

In the second case, the calculated value (1.261) is lesser than the table value (1.96) at 0.05 level of significance, showing that there is no significant difference between students studying in Government Aided and Self Finance Higher Secondary schools with regard to Sensitivity-a dimension of Social Intelligence.

In the third case, the calculated value (4.864) is greater than the expected table value (2.58) at 0.01 level of significance, showing that there is significant difference between students studying in Self finance and Government Higher Secondary schools with regard to Sensitivity-a dimension of Social Intelligence.

Moreover, students studying in Government Schools have exhibited significantly higher Sensitivity-a dimension of Social Intelligence than Government Aided and Self Finance school students.

Hence the hypothesis – 7 (b) stating that "There is no significant difference between the mean scores of Sensitivity -a dimension of Social Intelligence among Higher Secondary Students with regard to Type of Management of Schools" is partially verified.

INFLUENCE OF MEDIUM OF INSTRUCTION ON SENSITIVITY-A DIMENSION OF SOCIAL INTELLIGENCE

The scores related to Sensitivity -a dimension of Social Intelligence of Tamil and English medium Higher Secondary Students have been computed and details are furnished in the following table.

TABLE.9.35: Showing the Significant Difference between the mean Scores of Sensitivity -a Dimension of Social Intelligence with Respect to Medium of Instruction

Variable	Medium of Instruction	N	Mean	S.D	Critical Ratio	L.S
Sensitivity	Tamil	221	20.80	2.710	1.921	N.S
	English	79	20.04	3.791		

INFERENCE

From the table, it is clear that the obtained C. R value (1.921) is lower than the table value (1.96) at 0.05 level. Therefore there is no significant difference between the mean scores of Sensitivity -a dimension of social Intelligence among Higher Secondary Students with regard to Medium of Instruction.

Hence the hypothesis – 7 (c) stating that " There is no significant difference between the mean scores of Sensitivity -a dimension of Social Intelligence among Higher Secondary Students with regard to Medium of Instruction" is accepted.

INFLUENCE OF TYPE OF FAMILY ON SENSITIVITY-A DIMENSION OF SOCIAL INTELLIGENCE

The scores related to Sensitivity -a dimension of Social Intelligence of Higher Secondary Students hailing from Nuclear and Joint families have been computed and details are furnished in the following table.

TABLE.9.36: Showing the Significant Difference between the mean Scores of Sensitivity -a Dimension of Social Intelligence with Respect to Type of Family

Variable	Type of Family	N	Mean	S.D	Critical Ratio	L.S
Sensitivity	Nuclear	160	20.71	2.998	0.684	N.S
	Joint	140	20.47	3.101		

INFERENCE

From the table, it is clear that the obtained C.R value (0.684) is lesser than the table value (1.96) at 0.05 level. Therefore there is no significant difference between the mean scores of Sensitivity -a dimension of Social Intelligence among Higher Secondary Students with regard to Type of Family.

Hence the hypothesis –7 (d) stating that "There is no significant difference between the mean scores of Sensitivity -a dimension of Social Intelligence among Higher Secondary Students with regard to Type of Family" is accepted.

INFLUENCE OF LOCATION OF THE SCHOOL ON SENSITIVITY –A DIMENSION OF SOCIAL INTELLIGENCE

The scores related to Sensitivity -a dimension of Social Intelligence of Rural and Urban Higher Secondary Students have been computed and details are furnished in the following table.

TABLE. 9.37: Showing the Significant Difference between the mean Scores of Sensitivity -a Dimension of Social Intelligence with Respect to Location of the School

Variable	Location of the School	N	Mean	S.D	Critical Ratio	L.S
Sensitivity	Rural	100	19.82	2.907	3.186	0.01
	Urban	200	20.99	3.042		

INFERENCE

From the table, it is clear that the obtained C. R value (3.186) is greater than the table value (2.58) at 0.01 level. Therefore there is significant difference between the mean scores of Sensitivity -a dimension of Social Intelligence among Higher Secondary Students with regard to Location of the School. Urban students have significantly higher Sensitivity -a dimension of Social Intelligence than rural students.

Hence the hypothesis –7 (e) stating that "There is no significant difference between the mean scores of Sensitivity-a dimension of Social Intelligence among Higher Secondary Students with regard to Location of the School" is rejected.

INFLUENCE OF BIRTH ORDER ON SENSITIVITY-A DIMENSION OF SOCIAL INTELLIGENCE

The scores related to Sensitivity-a dimension of Social Intelligence of First born, Middle born and Last born Higher Secondary Students have been computed and details are furnished in the following table.

TABLE.9.38: ANOVA Showing the Significant Difference between the mean Scores of Sensitivity -a Dimension of Social Intelligence with Respect to Birth Order

Variable		Sum of Squares	df	Mean Squares	'F' Value	L.S
Sensitivity	Between Groups	82.687	2	41.343	4.569	0.05
	Within Groups	2687.313	297	9.048		
	Total	**2770.000**	**299**			

INFERENCE

From the table, it is clear that the obtained 'F' value (4.569) is greater than the table value (3.03) at 0.05 level. Therefore there is significant difference between the mean scores of Sensitivity -a dimension of Social Intelligence among Higher Secondary Students with regard to Birth Order. So, further analysis has been done between the groups.

TABLE.9.39: Showing the Mean, S.D and C.R value for Sensitivity -a Fimension of Social Intelligence of Higher Secondary Students based on Birth Order

Variable	Birth Order	F	Mean	Std Deviation	C.R Value	L.S
Sensitivity	First born Vs Middle born	101	20.49	3.315	1.896	N.S
		111	21.23	2.323		
	Middle bornVs Last born	111	21.23	2.323	3.164	0.01
		88	19.94	3.381		
	Last bornVs First born	88	19.94	3.381	1.111	N.S
		101	20.49	3.315		

INFERENCE

From the above table, following inferences have been made.

In the first case, the calculated value (1.896) is lower than table value (1.96) at 0.05 level of significance, showing that there is no significant difference between students studying in First born and Middle born Higher Secondary Students with regard to Sensitivity -a dimension of Social Intelligence.

In the second case, the calculated value (3.164) is higher than the table value (2.58) at 0.01 level of significance, showing that there is significant difference between students studying in Middle born and last born Higher Secondary Students with regard to Sensitivity -a dimension of Social Intelligence.

In the third case, the calculated value (1.111) is lesser than the expected table value (1.96) at 0.05 level of significance, showing that there is no significant difference between students studying in Last born and First born Higher Secondary Students with regard to Sensitivity -a dimension of Social Intelligence.

Moreover, Last born students have significantly lesser Sensitivity-a dimension of Social Intelligence than First born and Middle born students.

Hence the hypothesis – 7 (f) stating that "There is no significant difference between the mean scores of Sensitivity-a dimension of Social Intelligence among Higher Secondary Students with regard to Birth Order" is partially verified.

INFLUENCE OF GENDER ON RECOGNITION OF SOCIAL ENVIRONMENT-A DIMENSION OF SOCIAL INTELLIGENCE

The scores related to Recognition of Social Environment -a dimension of Social Intelligence of Male and Female Higher Secondary Students have been computed and details are furnished in the following table.

TABLE.9.40: Showing the Significant Difference between the mean Scores of Recognition of Social Environment -a Dimension of Social Intelligence with Respect to Gender

Variable	Gender	N	Mean	S.D	Critical Ratio	L.S
Recognition of Social Environment	Males	150	1.31	1.029	1.973	0.05
	Females	150	1.08	.959		

INFERENCE

From the table, it is clear that the obtained C. R value (1.973) is greater than the table value (1.96) at 0.05 level. Therefore there is significant difference between the mean scores of Recognition of Social Environment -a dimension of Social Intelligence among Higher Secondary Students with regard to Gender.

Boys have significantly higher Recognition of Social Environment -a dimension of Social Intelligence than their counter parts.

Hence the hypothesis – 8 (a) stating that " There is no significant difference between the mean scores of Recognition of Social Environment -a dimension of Social Intelligence among Higher Secondary Students with regard to Gender" is rejected.

INFLUENCE OF TYPE OF MANAGEMENT ON RECOGNITION OF SOCIAL ENVIRONMENT-A DIMENSION OF SOCIAL INTELLIGENCE

The scores related to Recognition of Social Environment -a dimension of Social Intelligence of Government, Government Aided and Self Finance Higher Secondary Students have been computed and details are furnished in the following table.

TABLE. 9.41: ANOVA Showing the Significant Difference between the mean Scores of Recognition of Social Environment-a Dimension Social Intelligence with Respect to Type of Management of Schools

Variable		Sum of Squares	df	Mean Squares	'F' Value	L.S
Recognition of Social Environment	Between Groups	74.647	2	37.323	49.456	0.01
	Within Groups	224.140	297	.755		
	Total	**298.787**	**299**			

INFERENCE

From the table, it is clear that the obtained 'F' value (49.456) is greater than the table value (4.68) at 0.01 level. Therefore there is significant difference between the mean scores of Recognition of Social Environment -a dimension of Social Intelligence among Higher Secondary Students with regard to Type of Management of Schools. So, further analysis has been done between the groups.

TABLE.9.42: Showing the Mean, S.D and C.R Value for Recognition of Social Environment -a Dimension of Social Intelligence of Higher Secondary Students based on Type of Management of Schools.

Variable	Type of Management of Schools	F	Mean	Std Deviation	C.R Value	L.S
Recognition of Social Environment	Government Vs Government Aided	100	.71	.756	2.410	0.05
		100	.99	.882		
	Government Aided Vs Self Finance	100	.99	.882	6.841	0.01
		100	1.88	.956		
	Self Finance Vs Government	100	1.88	.956	9.597	0.01
		100	.71	.756		

NFERENCE

From the above table, following inferences have been made.

In the first case, the calculated value (2.410) is greater than table value (1.96) at 0.05 level of significance, showing that there is significant difference between students studying in Government and Government Aided Higher Secondary schools with regard to Recognition of Social Environment -a dimension of Social Intelligence.

In the second case, the calculated value (6.841) is greater than the table value (2.58) at 0.01 level of significance, showing that there is significant difference between students studying in Government Aided and Self Finance of Higher Secondary schools with regard to Recognition of Social Environment -a dimension of Social Intelligence.

In the third case, the calculated value (9.597) is greater than the expected table value (2.58) at 0.01 level of significance, showing that there is significant difference between students studying in Self Finance and Government Higher Secondary schools with regard to Recognition of Social Environment -a dimension of Social Intelligence.

Moreover, Self Finance School students have significantly higher Recognition of Social Environment -a dimension of Social Intelligence than students studying in Goverment and Government Aided schools.

Hence the hypothesis – 8 (b) stating that "There is no significant difference between the mean scores of Recognition of Social Environment -a dimension of Social Intelligence among Higher Secondary Students with regard to Type of Management of Schools" is partially verified.

INFLUENCE OF MEDIUM OF INSTRUCTION ON RECOGNITION OF SOCIAL ENVIRONMENT -A DIMENSION OF SOCIAL INTELLIGENCE

The scores related to Recognition of Social Environment -a dimension of Social Intelligence of Tamil and English medium Higher Secondary Students have been computed and details are furnished in the following table.

TABLE.9.43: Showing the Significant Difference between the mean Scores of Recognition of Social Environment -a Dimension of Social Intelligence with Respect to Medium of Instruction

Variable	Medium of Instruction	N	Mean	S.D	Critical Ratio	L.S
Recognition of Social Environment	Tamil	221	1.06	.930	3.994	0.01
	English	79	1.57	1.094		

INFERENCE

From the table, it is clear that the obtained C.R value (3.994) is greater than the table value (2.58) at 0.01 level.Therefore there is significant difference between the mean scores of Recognition of Social Environment -a dimension of Social Intelligence among Higher Secondary Students with regard to Medium of Instruction.

Moeover, English medium students have significantly higher Recognition of Social Environment -a dimension of Social Intelligence than Tamil medium students.

Hence the hypothesis– 8 (c) stating that "There is no significant difference between the mean scores of Social environment -a dimension of Social Intelligence among Higher Secondary Students with regard to Medium of Instruction" is rejected.

INFLUENCE OF TYPE OF FAMILY ON RECOGNITION OF SOCIAL ENVIRONMENT-A DIMENSION OF SOCIAL INTELLIGENCE

The scores related to Recognition of Social Environment -a dimension of Social Intelligence of Higher Secondary Students hailing from Nuclear and Joint families have been computed and details are furnished in the following table.

TABLE.9.44: Showing the Significant Difference between the mean Scores of Recognition of Social Environment -a Dimension of Social Intelligence with Respect to Type of Family

Variable	Type of Family	N	Mean	S.D	Critical Ratio	L.S
Recognition of Social Environment	Nuclear	160	1.09	.967	1.970	0.05
	Joint	140	1.31	1.025		

INFERENCE

From the table, it is clear that the obtained C. R value (1.970) is greater than the table value (1.96) at 0.05 level. Therefore there is significant difference between the mean scores of Recognition of Social Environment -a dimension of Social Intelligence among Higher Secondary Students with regard to Type of Family.

Students hailing from Joint families have significantly higher Recognition of Social Environment -a dimension of Social Intelligence than Nuclear family students.

Hence the hypothesis – 8(d) stating that " There is no significant difference between the mean scores of Recognition of Social environment -a dimension of Social Intelligence among Higher Secondary Students with regard to Type of Family" is rejected.

INFLUENCE OF LOCATION OF THE SCHOOL ON RECOGNITION OF SOCIAL ENVIRONMENT -A DIMENSION OF SOCIAL INTELLIGENCE

The scores related to Recognition of Social Environment -a dimension of Social Intelligence of Rural and Urban Higher Secondary Students have been computed and details are furnished in the following table.

TABLE.9.45: Showing the Significant Difference between the mean Scores of Recognition of Social Environment -a Fimension of Social Intelligence with Respect to Location of the School

Variable	Location of the School	N	Mean	S.D	Critical Ratio	L.S
Recognition of Social Environment	Rural	100	1.88	.956	9.613	0.01
	Urban	200	.85	.831		

INFERENCE

From the table, it is clear that the obtained C. R value (9.613) is greater than the table value (2.58) at 0.01 level. Therefore there is significant difference between the mean scores of Recognition of Social Environment -a dimension of Social Intelligence among Higher Secondary Students with regard to Location of the School.

Rural students have significantly higher Recognition of Social Environment than urban students.

Hence the hypothesis – 8 (e) stating that "There is no significant difference between the mean scores of Recognition of Social Environment -a dimension of Social Intelligence among Higher Secondary Students with regard to Location of the School" is rejected.

INFLUENCE OF BIRTH ORDER ON RECOGNITION OF SOCIAL ENVIRONMENT -A DIMENSION OF SOCIAL INTELLIGENCE

The scores related to Recognition of Social Environment -a dimension of Social Intelligence of First born, Middle born and Last born Higher Secondary Students have been computed and details are furnished in the following table.

TABLE.9.46: ANOVA Showing the Significant Difference between the mean Scores of Recognition of Social Environment -a Dimension of Social Intelligence with Respect to Birth Order

Variable		Sum of Squares	df	Mean Squares	'F' Value	L.S
Recognition of Social Environment	Between Groups	4.312	2	2.156	2.174	N. S
	Within Groups	294.475	297	.991		
	Total	**298.787**	**299**			

INFERENCE

From the table, it is clear that the obtained 'F' value (2.174) is lower than the table value (3.03) at 0.05 level. Therefore there is no significant difference between the mean scores of Recognition of Social Environment -a dimension of Social Intelligence among Higher Secondary Students wih regard to Birth Order.

Hence the hypothesis – 8 (f) stating that "There is no significant difference between the mean scores of Recognition of Social Environment -a dimension of Social Intelligence among Higher Secondary Students with regard to Birth Order" is accepted.

INFLUENCE OF GENDER ON TACTFULNESS-A DIMENSION OF SOCIAL INTELLIGENCE

The scores related to Tactfulness-a dimension of Social Intelligence of Male and Female Higher Secondary Students have been computed and details are furnished in the following table.

TABLE.9.47: Showing the Significant Difference between the mean Scores of Tactfulness-a Dimension of Social Intelligence with Respect to Gender

Variable	Gender	N	Mean	S.D	Critical Ratio	L.S
Tactfulness	Males	150	3.96	1.510	.351	N.S
	Females	150	4.02	1.449		

INFERENCE

From the table, it is clear that the obtained C. R value (.351) is lower than the table value (1.96) at 0.05 level. Therefore there is no significant difference between the mean scores of Tactfulness-a dimension of Social Intelligence among Higher Secondary Students with regard to Gender.

Hence the hypothesis – 9 (a) stating that "There is no significant difference between the mean scores of Tactfulness-a dimension of Social Intelligence among Higher Secondary Students with regard to Gender" is accepted.

INFLUENCE OF TYPE OF MANAGEMENT OF SCHOOLS ON TACTFUL-NESS-A DIMENSION OF SOCIAL INTELLIGENCE

The scores related to Tactfulness-a dimension of Social Intelligence of Government, GovernmentAided and Selr finance Higher Secondary Students have been computed and details are furnished in the following table.

TABLE.9.48: ANOVA Showing the Significant Difference between the mean Scores of Tactfulness-a Dimension of Social Intelligence with Respect to Type of Management of Schools

Variable		Sum of Squares	df	Mean Squares	'F' Value	L.S
Tactfulness	Between Groups	92.580	2	46.290	24.533	0.01
	Within Groups	560.390	297	1.887		
	Total	**652.970**	**299**			

INFERENCE

From the table, it is clear that the obtained 'F' value (24.533) is greater than the table value (4.68) at 0.01 level. Therefore there is significant difference between the mean scores of Tactfulness-a dimension of Social Intelligence among Higher Secondary Students with regard to Type of Management of Schools. So, further analysis has been done between the groups.

TABLE.9.49: Showing the Mean, S.D and C.R value for Tactfulness-a Dimension of Social Intelligence of Higher Secondary Students based on Type of Management of Schools

Variable	Type of Management of Schools	F	Mean	Std Deviation	C.R Value	L.S
Tactfulness	Government Vs Government Aided	100	3.74	1.315	1.488	N.S
		100	3.47	1.251		
	Government Aided Vs Self Finance	100	3.47	1.251	6.507	0.01
		100	4.76	1.538		
	Self Finance Vs Government	100	4.76	1.538	5.040	0.01
		100	3.74	1.315		

INFERENCE

From the above table, following inferences have been made.

In the first case, the calculated value (1.488) is lesser than table value (1.96) at 0.05 level of significance, showing that there is no significant difference between students studying in Government and Government Aided Higher Secondary schools with regard to Tactfulness-a dimension of Social Intelligence.

In the second case, the calculated value (6.507) is greater than the table value (2.58) at 0.01 level of significance, showing that there is significant difference between students studying in Government Aided and Self Finance Higher Secondary schools with regard to Tactfulness-a dimension of Social Intelligence.

In the third case, the calculated value (5.040) is greater than the expected table value (2.58) at 0.01 level of significance, showing that there is significant difference between students studying in Self Finance and Government Higher Secondary schools with regard to Tactfulness-a dimension of Social Intelligence.

Moreover, Self Finance School students have significantly higher Tactfulness-a dimension of Social Intelligence than Government and Government Aided school students.

Hence the hypothesis – 9 (b) stating that "There is no significant difference between the mean scores of Tactfulness-a dimension of Social Intelligence among Higher Secondary Students with regard to Type of Management of Schools" is partially verified.

INFLUENCE OF MEDIUM OF INSTRUCTION ON TACTFULNESS -A DIMENSION OF SOCIAL INTELLIGENCE

The scores related to Tactfulness-a dimension of Social Intelligence of Tamil and English medium Higher Secondary Students have been computed and details are furnished in the following table.

TABLE.9.50: Showing the Significant Difference between the mean Dcores of Tactfulness-a Dimension of Social Intelligence with Respect to Medium of Instruction

Variable	Medium of Instruction	N	Mean	S.D	Critical Ratio	L.S
Tactfulness	Tamil	221	3.90	1.446	1.762	N.S
	English	79	4.24	1.546		

INFERENCE

From the table, it is clear that the obtained C. R value (1.762) is lower than the table value (1.96) at 0.05 level. Therefore there is no significant difference between the mean scores of Tactfulness-a dimension of Social Intelligence among Higher Secondary Students with regard to Medium of Instruction.

Hence the hypothesis – 9 (c) stating that "There is no significant difference between the mean scores of Tactfulness-a dimension of Social Intelligence among Higher Secondary Students with regard to Medium of Instruction" is accepted.

INFLUENCE OF TYPE OF FAMILY ON TACTFULNESS - A DIMENSION OF SOCIAL INTELLIGENCE

The scores related to Tactfulness-a dimension of Social Intelligence of Higher Secondary School Students hailing from Nuclear and Joint families have been computed and details are furnished in the following table.

TABLE.9.51: Showing the Significant Difference between the mean Scores of Tactfulness-a Dimension of Social Intelligence with Respect to Type of Family

Variable	Type of Family	N	Mean	S.D	Critical Ratio	L.S
Tactfulness	Nuclear	160	3.96	1.489	0.422	N.S
	Joint	140	4.03	1.469		

INFERENCE

From the table, it is clear that the obtained C.R value (0.422) is lesser than the table value (1.96)at 0.05 level.Therefore there is no significant difference between the mean scores of Tactfulness-a dimension of Social Intelligence among Higher Secondary Students with regard to Type of Family.

Hence the hypothesis – 9 (d) stating that " There is no significant difference between the mean scores of Tactfulness-a dimension of Social Intelligence among Higher Secondary Students with regard to Type of Family" is accepted.

INFLUENCE OF LOCATION OF THE SCHOOL ON TACTFULNESS - A DIMENSION OF SOCIAL INTELLIGENCE

The scores related to Tactfulness-a dimension of Social Intelligence of Rural and Urban Higher Secondary Students have been computed and details are furnished in the following table.

TABLE.9.52: Showing the Significant Difference between the mean Scores of Tactfulness-a Dimension of Social Intelligence with Respect to Location of the School

Variable	Location of the School	N	Mean	S.D	Critical Ratio	L.S
Tactfulness	Rural	100	4.76	1.538	6.855	0.01
	Urban	200	3.61	1.287		

INFERENCE

From the table, it is clear that the obtained C.R value (6.855) is greater than the table value (2.58) at 0.01 level. Therefore there is significant difference between the mean scores of Tactfulness-a dimension of Social Intelligence among Higher Secondary Students with regard to Location of the School. Rural students have significantly higher Tactfulness-a dimension of Social Intelligence than Urban students.

Hence the hypothesis – 9(e) stating that " There is significant difference between the mean scores of Tactfulness-a dimension of Social Intelligence among Higher Secondary Students with regard to Location of the School" is rejected.

INFLUENCE OF BIRTH ORDER ON TACTFULNESS -A DIMENSION OF SOCIAL INTELLIGENCE

The scores related to Tactfulness-a dimension of Social Intelligence of First born, Middle born and Last born Higher Secondary Students have been computed and details are furnished in the following table.

Table.9.53: ANOVA Showing the Significant Difference between the mean Scores of Tactfulness-a Dimension of Social Intelligence with Respect to Birth Order

Variable		Sum of Squares	df	Mean Squares	'F' Value	L.S
Tactfulness	Between Groups	.647	2	.323	0.147	N. S
	Within Groups	652.323	297	2.196		
	Total	652.970	299			

INFERENCE

From the table, it is clear that the obtained 'F' value (0.147) is lower than the table value (3.03) at 0.05 level. Therefore there is no significant difference between the mean scores of Tactfulness-a dimension of Social Intelligence among Higher Secondary Students with regard to Birth Order.

Hence the hypothesis – 9 (f) stating that "There is no significant difference between the mean scores of Tactfulness-a dimension of Social Intelligence among Higher Secondary Students with regard to Birth order" is accepted.

INFLUENCE OF GENDER ON SENSE OF HUMOUR -A DIMENSION OF SOCIAL INTELLIGENCE

The scores related to the Sense of Humour-a dimension of Social Intelligence of Male and Female Higher Secondary Students have been computed and details are furnished in the following table.

TABLE.9.54: Showing the Significant Difference between the mean Scores of the Sense of Humour-a Dimension of Social Intelligence with Respect to Gender

Variable	Gender	N	Mean	S.D	Critical Ratio	L.S
Sense of Humour	Males	150	3.43	1.884	.062	N.S
	Females	150	3.45	1.841		

INFERENCE

From the table, it is clear that the obtained C. R value (.062) is lower than the table value (1.96) at 0.05 level. Therefore there is no significant difference between the mean scores of the Sense of Humour-a dimension of Social Intelligence among Higher Secondary Students with regard to Gender.

Hence the hypothesis – 10 (a) stating that "There is no significant difference between the mean scores of the Sense of Humour-a dimension of Social Intelligence among Higher Secondary Students with regard to Gender" is accepted.

INFLUENCE OF TYPE OF MANAGEMENT OF SCHOOLS ON SENSE OF HUMOUR -A DIMENSION OF SOCIAL INTELLIGENCE

The scores related to the Sense of Humour-a dimension of Social Intelligence of Government, Government Aided and Self Finance Higher Secondary Students have been computed and details are furnished in the following table.

ABLE.9.55: ANOVA Showing the Significant Difference between the mean Scores of the Sense of Humour-a Dimension of Social Intelligence with Respect to Type of Management of Schools

Variable		Sum of Squares	df	Mean Squares	'F' Value	L.S
Sense of Humour	Between Groups	191.540	2	95.770	33.766	0.01
	Within Groups	842.380	297	2.836		
	Total	**1033.920**	**299**			

INFERENCE

From the table, it is clear that the obtained 'F' value (33.766) is greater than the table value (4.68) at 0.01 level. Therefore there is significant difference between the mean scores of the Sense of Humour-a dimension of Social Intelligence among Higher Secondary Students with regard to Type of Management of Schools. So, further analysis has been done between the groups.

TABLE.9.56: Showing the Mean, S.D and C.R value for the Sense of Humour-a Dimension of Social Intelligence of Higher Secondary Students based on Type of Management of Schools

Variable	Type of Management of Schools	N	Mean	Std Deviation	C.R Value	L.S
Sense of Humour	Government Vs Government Aided	100	2.88	1.387	.047	N.S
		100	2.87	1.625		
	Government Aided Vs Self Finance	100	2.87	1.625	6.625	0.01
		100	4.57	1.986		
	Self Finance Vs Government	100	4.57	1.986	6.976	0.01
		100	2.88	1.387		

INFERENCE

From the above table, following inferences have been made.

In the first case, the calculated value (.047) is lesser than table value (1.96) at 0.05 level of significance, showing that there is no significant difference between students studying in Government and Government Aided Higher Secondary schools with regard to the Sense of Humour-a dimension of Social Intelligence.

In the second case, the calculated value (6.625) is greater than the table value (2.58) at 0.01 level of significance, showing that there is significant difference between students studying in Government Aided and Self Finance of Higher Secondary schools with regard to the Sense of Humour-a dimension Social Intelligence.

In the third case, the calculated value (6.976) is greater than the expected table value (2.58) at 0.01 level of significance, showing that there is significant difference between students studying in Self Finance and Government Higher Secondary schools with regard to the Sense of Humour-a dimension of Social Intelligence.

Moreover, Self Finance school students have significantly higher Sense of Humour -a dimension of Social Intelligence than students studying in Government and Government Aided school students.

Hence the hypothesis – 10 (b) stating that "There is no significant difference between the mean scores of the Sense of Humour-a dimension of Social Intelligence among Higher Secondary Students with regard to Type of Management of Schools" is partially verified.

INFLUENCE OF MEDIUM OF INSTRUCTION ON SENSE OF HUMOUR -A DIMENSION OF SOCIAL INTELLIGENCE

The scores related to the Sense of Humour-a dimension of Social Intelligence of Tamil and English medium Higher Secondary Students have been computed and details are furnished in the following table.

TABLE.9.57: Showing the Significant Difference between the mean Scores of the Sense of Humour-a Dimension of Social Intelligence with Respect to Medium of Instruction

Variable	Medium of Instruction	N	Mean	S.D	Critical Ratio	L.S
Sense of Humour	Tamil	221	3.24	1.766	3.165	0.01
	English	79	4.00	2.006		

INFERENCE

From the table, it is clear that the obtained C.R value (3.165) is greater than the table value (2.58) at 0.01 level. Therefore there is significant difference between the mean scores of the Sense of Humour-a dimension of Social Intelligence among Higher Secondary students with regard to Medium of Instruction.

English medium students have significantly higher Sense of Humour-a dimension of Social Intelligence than Tamil medium students.

Hence the hypothesis –10 (c) stating that "There is no significant difference between the mean scores of the Sense of Humour-a dimension of Social Intelligence among Higher Secondary Students with regard to Medium of Instruction" is rejected.

INFLUENCE OF TYPE OF FAMILY ON SENSE OF HUMOUR-A DIMENSION OF SOCIAL INTELLIGENCE

The scores related to the Sense of Humour-a dimension of Social Intelligence of Higher Secondary Students hailing from Nuclear and Joint families have been computed and details are furnished in the following table.

TABLE.9.58: Showing the Significant Difference between the mean Scores of the Sense of Humour-a Dimension of Social Intelligence with Respect to Type of Family

Variable	Type of Family	N	Mean	S.D	Critical Ratio	L.S
Sense of Humour	Nuclear	160	3.15	1.727	2.924	0.01
	Joint	140	3.77	1.954		

INFERENCE

From the table, it is clear that the obtained C.R value (2.924) is greater than the table value (2.58) at 0.01 level. Therefore there is significant difference between the mean scores of the Sense of Humour-a dimension of Social Intelligence among Higher Secondary Students with regard to Type of Family.

Joint family students have significantly higher Sense of Humour than Nuclear family students.

Hence the hypothesis – 10 (d) stating that "There is significant difference between the mean scores of the Sense of Humour-a dimension of Social Intelligence among Higher Secondary Students with regard to Type of Family" is rejected.

INFLUENCE OF LOCATION OF THE SCHOOL ON SENSE OF HUMOUR-A DIMENSION OF SOCIAL INTELLIGENCE

The scores related to the Sense of Humour-a dimension of Social Intelligence of Rural and Urban Higher Secondary Students have been computed and details are furnished in the following table.

TABLE. 4.59: Showing the Significant Difference between the mean Scores of the Sense of Humour-Daimension of Social Intelligence with Respect to Location of the School

Variable	Location of the School	N	Mean	S.D	Critical Ratio	L.S
Sense of Humour	Rural	100	4.57	1.986	8.231	0.01
	Urban	200	2.88	1.507		

INFERENCE

From the table, it is clear that the obtained C. R value (8.231) is greater than the table value (2.58) at 0.01 level. Therefore there is significant difference between the mean scores of the Sense of Humour-a dimension of Social Intelligence among Higher Secondary Students with regard to Location of the School.

Rural students have significantly higher Sense of Humour-a dimension of Social Intelligence than Urban students.

Hence the hypothesis – 10 (e) stating that "There is no significant difference between the mean scores of the Sense of Humour-a dimension of Social Intelligence among Higher Secondary Students with regard to Location of the School" is rejected.

INFLUENCE OF BIRTH ORDER ON SENSE OF HUMOUR -A DIMENSION OF SOCIAL INTELLIGENCE

The scores related to the Sense of Humour-a dimension of Social Intelligence of First born ,Middle born and Last born Higher Secondary School Students have been computed and details are furnished in the following table.

TABLE.9.60: ANOVA Showing the Significant Difference between the mean Scores of the Sense of Humour-a Dimension of Social Intelligence with Respect to Birth Order

Variable		Sum of Squares	df	Mean Squares	'F' Value	L.S
Sense of Humour	Between Groups	16.991	2	8.496	2.481	N.S
	Within Groups	1016.929	297	3.424		
	Total	**1033.920**	**299**			

INFERENCE

From the table, it is clear that the obtained 'F' value (2.481) is lower than the table value (3.03) at 0.05 level. Therefore there is no significant difference between the mean scores of the Sense of Humour-a dimension of Social Intelligence among Higher Secondary Students with regard to Birth Order.

Hence the hypothesis – 10 (f) stating that "There is no significant difference between the mean scores of the Sense of Humour-a dimension of Social Intelligence among Higher Secondary Students with regard to Birth Order" is accepted.

INFLUENCE OF GENDER ON MEMORY -A DIMENSION OF SOCIAL INTELLIGENCE

The scores related to Memory-a dimension of Social Intelligence of Male and Female Higher Secondary Students have been computed and details are furnished in the following table.

TABLE.9.61: Showing the Significant Difference between the mean Scores of Memory-a Dimension of Social Intelligence with Respect to Gender

Variable	Gender	N	Mean	S.D	Critical Ratio	L.S
Memory	Males	150	10.18	2.114	1.543	N.S
	Females	150	9.83	1.842		

INFERENCE

From the table, it is clear that the obtained C. R value (1.543) is lower than the table value (1.96) at 0.05 level. Therefore there is no significant difference between the mean scores of Memory-a dimension of Social Intelligence among Higher Secondary Students with regard to Gender.

Hence the hypothesis –11(a) stating that "There is no significant difference between the mean scores of Memory-a dimension of social Intelligence among Higher Secondary Students with regard to Gender" is accepted.

INFLUENCE OF TYPE OF MANAGEMENT OF SCHOOLS ON MEMORY -A DIMENSION OF SOCIAL INTELLIGENCE

The scores related to Memory-a dimension of Social Intelligence of Government, Government Aided and Self Finance Higher Secondary Students have been computed and details are furnished in the following table.

TABLE.9.62: ANOVA Showing the Significant Difference between the mean Scores of Memory-a Dimension of Social Intelligence with Respect to Type of Management of SchoolsVariable

Variable		Sum of Squares	df	Mean Squares	'F' Value	L.S
Memory	Between Groups	28.687	2	14.343	3.697	0.05
	Within Groups	1152.310	297	3.880		
	Total	**1180.997**	**299**			

INFERENCE

From the table, it is clear that the obtained 'F' value (3.697) is greater than the table value (4.68) at 0.05 level. Therefore there is significant difference between the mean scores of Memory-a dimension of Social Intelligence among Higher Secondary Students with regard to Type of Management of Schools. So, further analysis has been done between the groups.

TABLE.9.63: Showing the Mean, S.D and C.R value for Memory-a Dimension of Social Intelligence of Higher Secondary Students based on Type of Management of Schools

Variable	Type of Management of Schools	N	Mean	Std Deviation	C.R Value	L.S
Memory	GovernmentVs Government Aided	100	9.58	2.345	2.575	0.05
		100	10.31	1.594		
	Government Aided Vs Self Finance	100	10.31	1.594	0.692	N.S
		100	10.12	1.898		
	Self Finance Vs Government	100	10.12	1.898	1.790	N.S
		100	9.58	2.345		

INFERENCE

From the above table, following inferences have been made.

In the first case, the calculated value (2.575) is greater than table value (1.96) at 0.05 level of significance, showing that there is significant difference between students studying in Government and Government Aided Higher Secondary schools with regard to Memory-a dimension of Social Intelligence.

In the second case, the calculated value (0.692) is lesser than the table value (1.96) at 0.05 level of significance, showing that there is no significant difference between students studying in Government Aided and Self Finance Higher Secondary schools with regard to Memory-a dimension of Social Intelligence.

In the third case, the calculated value (1.790) is lesser than the expected table value (1.96) at 0.05 level of significance, showing that there is no significant difference between students studying in Self Finance and Government Higher Secondary schools with regard to Memory-a dimension of Social Intelligence.

Moreover, Government School students have significantly lesser Memory than students studying in Government Aided and Self Finance schools.

Hence the hypothesis – 11 (b) stating that "There is no significant difference between the mean scores of Memory-a dimension of Social Intelligence among Higher Secondary Students with regard to Type of Management of Schools" is partially verified.

INFLUENCE OF MEDIUM OF INSTRUCTION ON MEMORY-A DIMENSION OF SOCIAL INTELLIGENCE

The scores related to Memory-a dimension of Social Intelligence of Tamil and English medium Higher Secondary Students have been computed and details are furnished in the following table.

TABLE.4.64: Showing the Significant Difference between the mean Scores of Memory-a Dimension of Social Intelligence with Respect to Medium of Instruction

Variable	Medium of Instruction	N	Mean	S.D	Critical Ratio	L.S
Memory	Tamil	221	9.86	2.013	2.173	0.05
	English	79	10.42	1.865		

NFERENCE

From the table, it is clear that the obtained C. R value (2.173) is greater than the table value (1.96) at 0.05 level. Therefore there is significant difference between the mean scores of Memory-a dimension of Social Intelligence among Higher Secondary Students with regard to Medium of Instruction. English medium students have exhibited significantly higher Memory than Tamil medium students.

Hence the hypothesis – 11 (c) stating that "There is no significant difference between the mean scores of Memory-a dimension of Social Intelligence among Higher Secondary Students with regard to Medium of Instruction" is rejected.

INFLUENCE OF TYPE OF FAMILY ON MEMORY -A DIMENSION OF SOCIAL INTELLIGENCE

The scores related to Memory-a dimension of Social Intelligence of Higher Secondary Students hailing from Nuclear and Joint families have been computed and details are furnished in the following table.

TABLE.9.65: Showing the Significant Difference between the mean Scores of Memory-a Dimension of Social Intelligence with Respect to Type of Family

Variable	Type of Family	N	Mean	S.D	Critical Ratio	L.S
Memory	Nuclear	160	9.94	2.099	0.554	N.S
	Joint	140	10.07	1.857		

INFERENCE

From the table, it is clear that the obtained C. R value (0.554) is lesser than the table value (1.96) at 0.05 level. Therefore there is no significant difference between the mean scores of Memory-a dimension of Social Intelligence among Higher Secondary Students with regard to Type of Family.

Hence the hypothesis –11(d) stating that " There is no significant difference between the mean scores of Memory-a dimension of Social Intelligence among Higher Secondary Students with regard to Type of Family" is accepted.

INFLUENCE OF LOCATION OF THE SCHOOL ON MEMORY -A DIMENSION OF SOCIAL INTELLIGENCE

The scores related to Memory-a dimension of Social Intelligence of Rural and Urban Higher Secondary Students have been computed and details are furnished in the following table.

TABLE.9.66: Showing the Significant Difference between the mean Scores of Memory-a Dimension of Social Intelligence with Respect to Location of the School

Variable	Location of the School	N	Mean	S.D	Critical Ratio	L.S
Memory	Rural	100	10.12	1.898	0.718	N.S
	Urban	200	9.95	2.033		

INFERENCE

From the table, it is clear that the obtained C. R value (0.718) is lesser than the table value (1.96) at 0.05 level. Therefore there is no significant difference between the mean scores of Memory-a dimension of Social Intelligence among Higher Secondary Students with regard to Location of the School.

Hence the hypothesis –11(e) stating that "There is no significant difference between the mean scores of Memory-a dimension of Social Intelligence among Higher Secondary Students with regard to Location of the School" is accepted.

INFLUENCE OF BIRTH ORDER ON MEMORY -A DIMENSION OF SOCIAL INTELLIGENCE

The scores related to Memory-a dimension of Social Intelligence of First born, Middle born and Last born Higher Secondary Students have been computed and details are furnished in the following table.

TABLE.9.67: ANOVA Showing the Significant Difference between the mean Scores of Memory-a Dimension of Social Intelligence with Respect to Birth Order

Variable		**Sum of Squares**	**df**	**Mean Squares**	**'F' Value**	**L.S**
Memory	Between Groups	3.495	2	1.747	0.441	N. S
	Within Groups	1177.502	297	3.965		
	Total	**1180.997**	**299**			

INFERENCE

From the table, it is clear that the obtained 'F' value (0.441) is lower than the table value (3.03) at 0.05 level. Therefore there is no significant difference between the mean scores of Memory-a dimension of Social Intelligence among Higher Secondary Students with regard to Birth Order.

Hence the hypothesis – 11(f) stating that "There is no significant difference between the mean scores of Memory-a dimension of Social Intelligence among Higher Secondary Students with regard to Birth Order" is accepted.

INFLUENCE OF GENDER ON SUBJECTIVE HAPPINESS

The scores related to Subjective Happiness of Male and Female Higher Secondary Students have been computed and details are furnished in the following table.

TABLE.9.68: Showing the Significant Difference between the mean Scores of Subjective Happiness with Respect to Gender

Variable	Gender	N	Mean	S.D	Critical Ratio	L.S
Subjective Happiness	Males	150	18.77	3.805	.231	N.S
	Females	150	18.67	3.681		

INFERENCE

From the table, it is clear that the obtained C. R value (0.231) is lower than the table value (1.96) at 0.05 level. Therefore there is no significant difference between the mean scores of Subjective Happiness among Higher Secondary Students with regard to Gender.

Hence the hypothesis – 12 (a) stating that "There is no significant differnce between the mean scores of Subjective Happiness among Higher Secondary Students with regard to Gender" is accepted.

INFLUENCE OF TYPE OF MANAGEMENT OF SCHOOLS ON SUBJECTIVE HAPPINESS

The scores related to Subjective Happiness of Government, Government Aided and Self Finance Higher Secondary Students have been computed and details are furnished in the following table.

TABLE.9.69: ANOVA Showing the Significant Difference between the mean Scores of Subjective Happiness with Respect to Type of Management of Schools

Variable		Sum of Squares	df	Mean Squares	'F' Value	L.S
Subjective Happiness	Between Groups	44.847	2	22.423	1.612	N.S
	Within Groups	4132.070	297	13.913		
	Total	4176.917	299			

INFERENCE

From the table, it is clear that the obtained 'F' value (1.612) is lesser than the table value (3.03) at 0.05 level. Therefore there is no significant difference between the mean scores of Subjective Happiness among Higher Secondary Students with regard to Type of Management of Schools.

Hence the hypothesis – 12 (b) stating that "There is no significant difference between the mean scores of Subjective Happiness among Higher Secondary Students with regard to Type of Management of Schools" is accepted.

INFLUENCE OF MEDIUM OF INSTRUCTION ON SUBJECTIVE HAPPINESS

The scores related to Subjective Happiness of Tamil and English medium Higher Secondary Students have been computed and details are furnished in the following table.

TABLE.9.70: Showing the Significant Difference between the mean Scores of Subjective Happiness with Respect to Medium of Instruction

Variable	Medium of Instruction	N	Mean	S.D	Critical Ratio	L.S
Subjective Happiness	Tamil	221	18.67	3.983	.364	N.S
	English	79	18.85	2.962		

INFERENCE

From the table, it is clear that the obtained C. R value (0.364) is lesser than the table value (1.96) at 0.05 level. Therefore there is no significant difference between the mean scores of Subjective Happiness among Higher Secondary Students with regard to Medium of Instruction.

Hence the hypothesis –12(c) stating that "There is no significant difference between the mean scores of Subjective Happiness among Higher Secondary Students with regard to Medium of Instruction" is accepted.

INFLUENCE OF TYPE OF FAMILY ON SUBJECTIVE HAPPINESS

The scores related to Subjective Happiness of Higher Secondary Students hailing from Nuclear and Joint families have been computed and details are furnished in the following table.

TABLE.9.71: Showing the Significant Difference between the mean Scores of Subjective Happiness with Respect to Type of Family

Variable	Type of Family	N	Mean	S.D	Critical Ratio	L.S
Subjective Happiness	Nuclear	160	18.52	3.748	.846	N.S
	Joint	140	18.89	3.732		

INFERENCE

From the table, it is clear that the obtained C. R value (.846) is lower than the table value (1.96) at 0.05 level. Therefore there is no significant difference between the mean scores of Subjective Happiness among Higher Secondary Students with regard to Type of Family.

Hence the hypothesis – 12(d) stating that "There is no significant difference between the mean scores of Subjective Happiness among Higher Secondary Students with regard to Type of Family" is accepted.

INFLUENCE OF LOCATION OF THE SCHOOL ON SUBJECTIVE HAPPINESS

The scores related to Subjective Happiness of Rural and Urban Higher Secondary Students have been computed and details are furnished in the following table.

TABLE.9.72: Showing the Significant Difference between the mean Scores of Subjective Happiness with Respect to Location of the School

Variable	Location of the School	N	Mean	S.D	Critical Ratio	L.S
Subjective Happiness	Rural	100	18.82	3.474	.338	N.S
	Urban	200	18.67	3.870		

INFERENCE

From the table, it is clear that the obtained C. R value (.338) is lesser than the table value (1.96) at 0.05 level. Therefore there is no significant difference between the mean scores of Subjective Happiness among Higher Secondary Students with regard to Location of the School.

Hence the hypothesis – 12(e) stating that "There is no significant difference between the mean scores of Subjective Happiness among Higher Secondary Students with regard to Location of the school" is accepted.

INFLUENCE OF BIRTH ORDER ON SUBJECTIVE HAPPINESS

The scores related to Subjective Happiness of First born, Middle born and Last born Higher Secondary Students have been computed and details are furnished in the following table.

TABLE.9.73: ANOVA Showing the Significant Difference between the mean Scores of Subjective Happiness with Respect to Birth Order

Variable		Sum of Squares	df	Mean Squares	'F' Value	L.S
Subjective Happiness	Between Groups	131.135	2	65.567	4.813	0.01
	Within Groups	4045.782	297	13.622		
	Total	**4176.917**	**299**			

INFERENCE

From the table, it is clear that the obtained 'F' value (4.813) is greater than the table value (4.68) at 0.01 level. Therefore there is significant difference between the mean scores of Subjective Happiness among Higher Secondary Students with regard to Birth Order.

So, further analysis has been done between the groups.

TABLE.9.74: Showing the Mean, S.D and C.R value for Subjective Happiness of Higher Secondary Students based on Birth Order

Variable	Birth Order	F	Mean	Std Deviation	C.R Value	L.S
Subjective Happiness	First born Vs Middle born	101	18.22	4.112	.269	N.S
		111	18.36	3.595		
	Middle born Vs Last born	111	18.36	3.595	2.793	0.01
		88	19.74	3.275		
	Last born Vs First born	88	19.74	3.275	2.784	0.01
		101	18.22	4.112		

INFERENCE

From the above table, following inferences have been made.

In the first case, the calculated value (.269) is lower than table value (1.96) at 0.05 level of significance, showing that there is no significant difference between First born and Middle born students with regard to Subjective Happiness.

In the second case, the calculated value (2.793) is higher than the table value (2.58) at 0.01 level of significance, showing that there is significant difference between Middle born and last born students with regard to Subjective Happiness .

In the third case, the calculated value (2.784) is greater than the expected table value (2.58) at 0.01 level of significance, showing that there is significant difference between Last born and First born students with regard to Subjective Happiness.

Moreover,Last born students have significantly higher Subjective Happiness than First born and Middle born students.

Hence the hypothesis – 12(f) stating that " There is no significant difference between the mean scores of Subjective Happiness among Higher Secondary Students with regard to Birth Order" is partially verified.

RELATION BETWEEN THE SOCIAL INTELLIGENCE AND SUBJECTIVE HAPPINESS

The scores related to correlation between the Social Intelligence and Subjective Happiness of Higher Secondary Students have been computed and details are furnished in the following table.

TABLE.9.75: Showing the Correlation between Social Intelligence and Subjective Happiness

Variable	N	'r' Value	L.S
Social Intelligence and Subjective Happiness	300	0.236	0.05

INFERENCE

From the above table, it is clearly observed that the 'r' value (0.236) is greater than the table value (0.113) at 0.05 level. So there is significant correlation between Social Intelligence and Subjective Happiness among Higher Secondary Students.

Hence the hypothesis -13 stating that " There is no significant correlation between Social Intelligence and Subjective Happiness among Higher Secondary Students" is rejected.

CONCLUSION

The analysis and interpretation of data represent the application of deductive and inductive logic to the research process. A brief report of the present research study together with major finding and conclusion has been presented in the succeeding chapter.

❐

10

Summary, Findings and Conclusion

In this chapter, a brief summary of the study stating the problem, the objectives and the hypotheses, the methodology and the major findings are presented. The educational implications of the study are discussed, suggesting a few areas for further research.

STATEMENT OF THE PROBLEM

The title of the problem is as follows:

- A Critical Study on Social Intelligence of Higher Secondary Students Leading to Their Subjective Happiness.

OBJECTIVES OF THE STUDY

The following objectives have been set in the present study.

1. To find out the level of Social Intelligence of Higher Secondary Students.
2. To find out the level of Subjective Happiness of Higher Secondary Students.
3. To find out whether there is any significant difference in Social Intelligence and its dimension among Higher Secondary Students with regard to

Gender	:	Male/Female
Type of Management of Schools	:	Government/ Government Aided/Self Finance Schools
Medium of Instruction	:	Tamil/English
Type of Family	:	Nuclear/Joint
Location of the School	:	Rural/Urban
Birth order	:	First born/Middle born/Last born

4. To find out whether there is any significant difference in Subjective Happiness among Higher Secondary Students with regard to

Gender	:	Male/Female
Type of Management of Schools	:	Government/Government Aided/Self Finance Schools
Medium of Instruction	:	Tamil/English
Type of Family	:	Nuclear/Joint
Location of the School	:	Rural/Urban
Birth order	:	First born/Middle born/Last born

5. To find out whether there is any significant correlation between Social Intelligence of Higher Secondary Students and their Subjective Happiness.

HYPOTHESES OF THE STUDY

The hypotheses formed in the present study are listed below:

1. The level of Social Intelligence of Higher Secondary Students is average in nature.
2. The level of Subjective Happiness of Higher Secondary Students is average in nature.
3. There is no significant difference in Social Intelligence among Higher Secondary Students with regard to

Gender	:	Male/Female
Type of Management of Schools	:	Government/Government Aided/Self Finance Schools
Medium of Instruction	:	Tamil/English
Type of Family	:	Nuclear/Joint
Location of the School	:	Rural/Urban
Birth order	:	First born/Middle born/Last born

4. There is no significant difference in Patience - a dimension of Social Intelligence among Higher Secondary Students with regard to

Gender	: Male/Female
Type of Management of Schools	: Government/Government Aided/Self Finance Schools
Medium of Instruction	: Tamil/English
Type of Family	: Nuclear/Joint
Location of the School	: Rural/Urban
Birth order	: First born/Middle born/Last born

5. There is no significant difference in Co - operativeness - a dimension of Social Intelligence among Higher Secondary Students with regard to

Gender	: Male/Female
Type of Management of Schools	: Government/Government Aided/Self Finance Schools
Medium of Instruction	: Tamil/English
Type of Family	: Nuclear/Joint
Location of the School	: Rural/Urban
Birth order	: First born/Middle born/Last born

6. There is no significant difference in Confidence level - a dimension of Social Intelligence among Higher Secondary Students with regard to

Gender	: Male/Female
Type of Management of Schools	: Government/Government Aided/Self Finance Schools
Medium of Instruction	: Tamil/English
Type of Family	: Nuclear/Joint
Location of the School	: Rural/Urban
Birth order	: First born/Middle born/Last born

7. There is no significant difference in Sensitivity - a dimension of Social Intelligence among Higher Secondary Students with regard to

Gender	: Male/Female
Type of Management of Schools	: Government/ Government Aided/Self Finance Schools
Medium of Instruction	: Tamil/English
Type of Family	: Nuclear/Joint
Location of the School	: Rural/Urban
Birth order	: First born/Middle born/Last born

8. There is no significant difference in Recognition of Social Environment - a dimension of Social Intelligence among Higher Secondary Students with regard to

Gender	:	Male/Female
Type of Management of Schools	:	Government/ Government Aided/Self Finance Schools
Medium of Instruction	:	Tamil/English
Type of Family	:	Nuclear/Joint
Location of the School	:	Rural/Urban
Birth order	:	First born/Middle born/Last born

9. There is no significant difference in Tactfulness - a dimension of Social Intelligence among Higher Secondary Students with regard to

Gender	:	Male/Female
Type of Management of Schools	:	Government/ Government Aided/Self Finance Schools
Medium of Instruction	:	Tamil/English
Type of Family	:	Nuclear/Joint
Location of the School	:	Rural/Urban
Birth order	:	First born/Middle born/Last born

10. There is no significant difference in Sense of Humour - a dimension of Social Intelligence among Higher Secondary Students with regard to

Gender	:	Male/Female
Type of Management of Schools	:	Government/Government Aided/Self Finance Schools
Medium of Instruction	:	Tamil/English
Type of Family	:	Nuclear/Joint
Location of the School	:	Rural/Urban
Birth order	:	First born/Middle born/Last born

11. There is no significant difference in Memory - a dimension of Social Intelligence among Higher Secondary Students with regard to

Gender	:	Male/Female
Type of Management of Schools	:	Government/Government Aided/Self Finance Schools
Medium of Instruction	:	Tamil/English
Type of Family	:	Nuclear/Joint

Location of the School	:	Rural/Urban
Birth order	:	First born/Middle born/Last born

12. There is no significant difference in Subjective Happiness among Higher Secondary Students with regard to

Gender	:	Male/Female
Type of Management of Schools	:	Government/Government Aided/Self Finance Schools
Medium of Instruction	:	Tamil/English
Type of Family	:	Nuclear/Joint
Location of the School	:	Rural/Urban
Birth order	:	First born/Middle born/Last born

13. There is no significant correlation between social Intelligence and Subjective Happiness of Higher Secondary Students.

SAMPLE OF THE STUDY

Data was collected from the Higher Secondary Students adopting Stratified Random Sampling method. The total sample size was 300 drawn from 3 schools were selected for the study belonging to different Types of Management of Schools: *Government,* Government *Aided and Self Finance* schools

TOOLS USED FOR THE PRESENT STUDY

1. Social Intelligence scale constructed by Dr.N.K.chadha and Ms.Usha Ganesan(2005)
2. Subjective Happiness Scale constructed by Sonja Lyumbomirsky(2010).

MAJOR FINDINGS

The following findings have been arrived at based on present investigation.

1. The level of Social Intelligence of Higher Secondary Students is moderate in nature.
2. The level of Subjective Happiness of Higher Secondary Students is moderate in nature.
3. There is significant difference between the mean scores of Social Intelligence among higher secondary students with regard to Gender. Female students have higher Social Intelligence than their counterparts.
4. There is significant difference between the mean scores of Social Intelligence among Higher Secondary Students with regard to Type of Management of Schools. Government school students have significantly higher Social Intelligence than the students studying in Government Aided and Self Finance schools.

5. There is no significant difference between the mean scores of Social Intelligence among Higher Secondary Students with regard to Medium of Instruction.
6. There is no significant difference between the mean scores of Social Intelligence among Higher Secondary Students with regard to Type of Family.
7. There is no significant difference between the mean scores of Social Intelligence among Higher Secondary Students regards to Location of the school .
8. There is significant difference between the mean scores of Social Intelligence among Higher Secondary Students with regard to Birth Order.Middle born students have exhibited significantly higher Social Intelligence than First born and Last born students.
9. There is significant difference between the mean scores of Patience-a dimension of social Intelligence among Higher Secondary Students with regard to Gender.Female students have significantly Higher Patience-a dimension of Social Intelligence than their counter parts.
10. There is significant difference between the mean scores of Patience-a dimension of Social Intelligence among Higher Secondary Students with regard to Type of Management of Schools. Government School students have significantly higher Patience-a dimension of Social Intelligence than Government Aided and Self Finance school students.
11. There is significant difference between the mean scores of Patience-a dimension of Social Intelligence among Higher Secondary Students with regard to Medium of Instruction.Tamil medium students have significantly higher Patience-a dimension of Social Intelligence than their English medium students.
12. There is no significant difference between the mean scores of Patience-a dimension of Social Intelligence among Higher Secondary Students with regard to Type of family.
13. There is significant difference between the mean scores of Patience-a dimension of Social Intelligence among Higher Secondary Students with regard to Location of the School.Urban students have significantly higher Patience –a dimension of Social Intelligence than Rural students.
14. There is no significant difference between the mean scores of Patience-a dimension of Social Intelligence among Higher Secondary Students with regard to Birth Order.
15. There is significant difference between the mean scores of Co-operativeness-a dimension Social Intelligence among Higher Secondary

Students with regard to Gender.Girls have significantly higher Co-operativeness-a dimension of Social Intelligence than their counter parts.

16. There is significant difference between the mean scores of Co-operativeness-a dimension of Social Intelligence among Higher Secondary Students with regard to Type of Management of Schools. Government school students have significantly higher Co-operativeness -a dimension of Social Intelligence than in Government Aided and Self Finance school students.
17. There is no significant difference between the mean scores of Co-operativeness-a dimension of Social Intelligence among Higher Secondary Students with regard to Medium of Instruction.
18. There is no significant difference between the mean scores of Co-operativeness-a dimension of Social Intelligence among Higher Secondary Students with regard to Type of Family.
19. There is no significant difference between the mean scores of Co-operativeness-a dimension of Social Intelligence among Higher Secondary Students with regard to Location of the School .
20. There is no significant difference between the mean scores of Social Intelligence among Higher Secondary Students with regard to Birth Order.
21. There is significant difference between the mean scores of Confidence Level -a dimension of Social Intelligence among Higher Secondary Students with regard to Gender.Female students have significantly higher Confidence Level -a dimension of Social Intelligence than their counter parts.
22. There is significant difference between the mean scores of Confidence Level -a dimension of Social Intelligence among Higher Secondary Students with regard to Type of Management of Schools.Government School students have significantly higher Confidence Level than students studying in Government Aided and Self Finance schools.
23. There is significant difference between the mean scores of Confidence-a dimension of Social Intelligence among Higher Secondary Students with regard to Medium of Instruction.Tamil medium students have significantly higher Confidence Level than their counter parts.
24. There is no significant difference between the mean scores of Confidence Level -a dimension of Social Intelligence among Higher Secondary Students with regard to Type of Family.
25. There is significant difference between the mean scores of Confidence Level -a dimension of Social Intelligence among Higher Secondary

Students with regard to Location of the School.Urban students have significantly higher confidence Level -a dimension of Social Intelligence than Rural students.

26. There is no significant difference between the mean scores of Confidence Level -a dimension of Social Intelligence among Higher Secondary Students with regard to Birth Order.
27. There is significant difference between the mean scores of Sensitivity -a dimension of Social Intelligence among Higher Secondary Students with regard to Gender.Girls have significantly higher Sensitivity -a dimension of Social Intelligence than their counter parts.
28. There is significant difference between the mean scores of Sensitivity -a dimension of Social Intelligence among Higher Secondary Students with regard to Type of Management of Schools. Students studying in Government schools have exhibited significantly higher Sensitivity-a dimension of Social Intelligence than Government Aided and Self Finance school students.
29. There is no significant difference between the mean scores of Sensitivity -a dimension of Social Intelligence among Higher Secondary Students with regard to Medium of Instruction.
30. There is no significant difference between the mean scores of Sensitivity -a dimension of Social Intelligence among Higher Secondary Students with regard to Type of Family.
31. There is significant difference between the mean scores of Sensitivity -a dimension of Social Intelligence among Higher Secondary Students with regard to Location of the School.Urban students have significantly higher Sensitivity -a dimension of Social Intelligence than Rural students.
32. There is significant difference between the mean scores of Sensitivity -a dimension of Social Intelligence among Higher Secondary Students with regard to Birth Order. Last born students have significantly lesser Sensitivity -a dimension of Social Intelligence than First born and Middle born students.
33. There is significant difference between the mean scores of Recognition of Social Environment -a dimension of Social Intelligence among Higher Secondary Students with regard to Gender.Boys have significantly higher Recognition of Social Environment -a dimension of Social Intelligence than their counter parts.
34. There is significant difference between the mean scores of Recognition of Social Environment -a dimension of Social Intelligence among Higher Secondary Students with regard to Type of Management

of Schools. Self Finance school students have significantly higher Recognition of Social Environment -a dimension of Social Intelligence than students studying in Goverment And Government Aided schools.

35. There is significant difference between the mean scores of Recognition of Social Environment -a dimension of Social Intelligence among Higher Secondary Students with regard to Medium of Instruction. English medium students have significantly higher Recognition of Social Environment -a dimension of Social Intelligence than Tamil medium students.
36. There is significant difference between the mean scores of Recognition of Social Environment -a dimension of Social Intelligence among Higher Secondary Students with regard to Type of Family. Students hailing from Joint families have significantly higher Recognition of Social Environment -a dimension of Social Intelligence than Nuclear family students.
37. There is significant difference between the mean scores of Recognition Social Environment -a dimension of Social Intelligence among Higher Secondary Students with regard to Location of the School.Rural students have significantly higher Recognition of Social Environment than urban students.
38. There is no significant difference between the mean scores of Recognition of Social Environment -a dimension of Social Intelligence among higher secondary students wih regard to Birth Order.
39. There is no significant difference between the mean scores of Tactfulness-a dimension of Social Intelligence among Higher Secondary Students with regard to Gender.
40. There is significant difference between the mean scores of Tactfulness-a dimension of Social Intelligence among Higher Secondary Students with regard to Type of Management of Schools. Self Finance School students have significantly higher Tactfulness-a dimension of Social Intelligence than Government and Government Aided school students.
41. There is no significant difference between the mean scores of Tactfulness-a dimension of Social Intelligence among Higher Secondary Students with regard to Medium of Instruction.
42. There is no significant difference between the mean scores of Tactfulness-a dimension of Social Intelligence among Higher Secondary Students with regard to Type of Family.
43. There is significant difference between the mean scores of Tactfulness-a dimension of Social Intelligence among Higher Secondary Students with regard to Location of the School.Rural students have significantly

higher Tactfulness-a dimension of Social Intelligence than Urban students.

44. There is no significant difference between the mean scores of Tactfulness -a dimension of Social Intelligence among Higher Secondary Students with regard to Birth Order.
45. There is no significant difference between the mean scores of the Sense of Humour-a dimension of Social Intelligence among Higher Secondary Students with regard to Gender.
46. There is significant difference between the mean scores of the Sense of Humour-a dimension of Social Intelligence among Higher Secondary Students with regard to Type of Management of Schools. Self Finance school students have significantly higher Sense of Humour -a dimension of Social Intelligence than students studying in Government and Government Aided school students.
47. There is significant difference between the mean scores of the Sense of Humour-a dimension of Social Intelligence among Higher Secondary Students with regard to Medium of Instruction. English medium students have significantly higher Sense of Humour-a dimension of Social Intelligence than Tamil medium students.
48. There is significant difference between the mean scores of the Sense of Humour-a dimension of Social Intelligence among Higher Secondary Students with regard to Type of Family.Joint family students have significantly higher Sense of Humour than Nuclear family students.
49. There is significant difference between the mean scores of the Sense of Humour-a dimension of Social Intelligence among Higher Secondary Students with regard to Location of the School.Rural students have significantly higher Sense of Humour-a dimension of Social Intelligence than Urban students.
50. There is no significant difference between the mean scores of the Sense of Humour-a dimension of Social Intelligence among Higher Secondary Students with regard to Birth Order.
51. There is no significant difference between the mean scores of Memory-a dimension of Social Intelligence among Higher Secondary Students with regard to Gender
52. There is significant difference between the mean scores of Memory-a dimension of Social Intelligence among Higher Secondary Students with regard to Type of Management of Schools. Government School students have significantly lesser Memory than students studying in Government Aided and Self Finance schools.

53. There is significant difference between the mean scores of Memory-a dimension of Social Intelligence among Higher Secondary Students with regard to Medium of Instruction.English medium students have exhibited significantly higher Memory than Tamil medium students.
54. There is no significant difference between the mean scores of Memory-a dimension of Social Intelligence among Higher Secondary Students with regard to Type of Family.
55. There is no significant difference between the mean scores of Memory-a dimension of Social Intelligence among Higher Secondary Students with regard to Location of the School.
56. There is no significant difference between the mean scores of Memory-a dimension of Social Intelligence among Higher Secondary Students with regard to Birth Order.
57. There is no significant difference between the mean scores of Subjective Happiness among Higher Secondary Students with regard to Gender.
58. There is no significant difference between the mean scores of Subjective Happiness among Higher Secondary Students with regard to Type of Management of Schools.
59. There is no significant difference between the mean scores of Subjective Happiness among Higher Secondary Students with regard to Medium of Instruction.
60. There is no significant difference between the mean scores of Subjective Happiness among Higher Secondary Students with regard to Type of Family.
61. There is no significant difference between the mean scores of Subjective Happiness among Higher Secondary Students with regard to Location of the School.
62. There is significant difference between the mean scores of Subjective Happiness among Higher Secondary Students with regard to Birth Order. Last born students have significantly higher Subjective Happiness than First born and Middle born students.
63. There is significant correlation between Social Intelligence and Subjective Happiness among Higher Secondary Students.

EDUCATIONAL IMPLICATIONS & RECOMMENDATIONS

The findings of the present investigation are important for the improvement of the Quality of education. Social Intelligence being an important aspect of human behavior, throws light on the behavior of the Higher Secondary Students .Social Intelligence is also an ability which plays a major role in life. The following are some of the major recommendations to improve the Social

Intelligence and Subjective Happiness of the students.

Parents could be the proper motivator to develop Social Intelligence among the school students by the process of guiding, directing, stimulating and encouraging at every step.

Most of the programmes in Schools are heavily oriented towards information sharing, rather than encouraging and developing Social Intelligence. Therefore it is a felt need to review and modify the programmes in colleges.

Social Intelligence helps the students to improve their self or worth value and develop the right attitude towards society and this in future would help them to become better people. This positive attitude automatically increases their problem solving ability. This increases in Subjective Happiness also and helps the students to mould themselves to a better personality.

This further helps them to be flexible with their friends and fellow beings which pave the way for unity in diversity. Since teachers play a vital role in the development process of any individual, early identification and environment stimulation related to improve Social Intelligence can be provided. The teachers should adopt modern teaching strategies and methods in the class room to give opportunities for the enhancement of these qualities by organizing workshops, conference, seminars and also including the aspect within the curriculum among the schools.

Development of Social intelligence among school students is a different complex task. In schools there should be lot of scope for participation in different programme, curricular and co-curricular activities. Children should be encouraged to participate in all programmes, since they offer scope for developing Flexible manner, Tolerence and Self evaluation ability among the individuals.

Our particular interest is in the possible benefits of high Subjective happiness and corresponding costs of low Subjective happiness .This is not only possible theoretical perspective, but it is the one that has characterized the Subjective happiness movement indeed our own initial interest is Subjective happiness. Does high Subjective happiness make life better? Should parents, teachers or others seek to boost Subjective happiness, whenever possible? High Subjective happiness may be the result of doing well in school. People high in Subjective happiness regard themselves as better liked and more popular than others, but most of these advantages exist mainly in their minds, and objective data generally fail to confirm them.

Subjective happiness and social Intelligence are positively related in this study. If the students are high in social Intelligence, then they will be having Subjective happiness.

LIMITATIONS

1. The study was restricted to Thiruvannamalai District of Tamil Nadu.
2. Number of samples was confined to 300.
3. The research is concentrated on three types of schools Government, Government Aided, and Self Finance schools.
4. Only class (+1) level student from Higher Secondary Schools were taken for the study.

SUGGESTIONS FOR FURTHER RESEARCH

Some suggestions with regard to possibilities of the research in the field of education are offered with a view to stimulate prospective research workers in this area.

- This study was conducted only to XIth class students and can be extended to college level.
- The present study is limited to schools in Thiruvannamalai.
- The present study has done only in some schools at Thiruvannamalai District; similar study comprising different districts can be attempted.
- A comparative study between Subjective Happiness and Social Intelligence can also be done in further studies.

CONCLUSION

The purpose of the present study was to study the relationship among the variables like Subjective happiness, and Social Intelligence. The study is sure to find some usefulness in the field of education and findings of the study can serve as a database for further research.

❒

11

Awareness on Environmental Education

EDUCATION

Education for all children is a prime goal of our Indian democracy. Education is a basic request for responsible citizenship, maintenance of our life and for successful entry into today's complex world of work. In our country, Education is freely available, yet an alarmingly large number of intellectually capable children leave school education. They are wasting their mental capacities dissipating their opportunities and circumscribing their chances for a better life.

Schooling is the major task of the adolescent just as earning. In the present system of Education, it is the elementary stage which is the most crucial stage of education as it lays the foundation for the personality attitudes, self-confidence labia, learning skills and to scope with the difficulties of real life situations secondary education is also more valuable and it is the platform to foster and develop economical and societal growth. A major challenge is to given better and quality education.

The progress of a nation in the world of today is more than ever dependent upon the quantity and quality of education reviewed by people. From the point of view of Education, as a human need, emphasis has to be placed on the mastery of the spoken word as a medium of communication and socialization the acquisition of universal literacy, its capitalization, the acquisition of universal elementary and secondary education on a part time are full time basis and as a life-long activity. Education as a basic human need, therefore, opens unlimited possibilities calling for responses that are constructive, creative and challenging.

In most of the countries, there is widespread acceptance of the principle that Education is fundamental human rights. Education is fundamental to all rural development of human potential, material and spirit, thus furthering the goal of socialism, secularism and democracy enshrined in our constitution. Education develops manpower for different levels of economy and empowers the poor masses to become self reliant enough to participate in the process of national development. Education is thus an instrument for developing an economically prosperous society and for ensuring security and social justice.

Education is the soul of human civilization and development which is lacking among the people. To complete with general communities, it is necessary to equip them educationally. As per general perception, the schooling system offers the children and opportunity. On equal terms with others to gain knowledge and enable them to rise in socio-economic status.

Education is to be complete must have five Principal aspects relating to the five principal activities of human beings. The physical the mental, the social, the emotional and the spiritual. Usually these phases of education succeed each other in a chronological order following the growth of the individual.

The term ‘education’, as a learning process implies acquiring knowledge. Education cannot “Modification of human behaviour” or “drawing out the best in man” and it is a lifelong process which cannot be confined only to four walls of the schools or colleges. Education aims at the total and wholesome or harmonious development of the personality of the child: it should afford opportunities to the individual to develop physically, mentally, intellectually, morally and socially education makes man rational. Self-reliant, self-conscious, civilized, sociable and harmonious. It inculcates good habits in man and makes his life systematic, develops aspirations ambitions and desires in him, makes him powerful and paves the way for his development.

IMPORTANCE OF EDUCATION

1. Education is the special manifestation of men.
2. It is the treasure which can be preserved without fear of loss.
3. It secures materials pleasure, happiness.
4. It secures honour at the hands of state not money.

5. Learning is an excellence of wealth that none destroy to man. To man naught else affords reality of joy.
6. The fundamental purpose of education is the same of all times and in all places.
7. Education is a preparation for a living and life.

ENVIRONMENTAL EDUCATION

The word Environment is derived from the French word 'Environ' meaning 'surroundings'. Each and everything around us is called as environment. Every organism is surrounded by materials and forces which constitute its environment from which it must derive its needs. Environment creates favourable conditions for the existence and deployment of living organisms.

Environment is the concern of mankind. We all wish to have a clean environment but very few of us are aware and much less feel genuinely concerned about it. Environment is the sum total of substances and forces around any organisms, affecting its very existence.

Environmental education refers to organized efforts to teach about how natural environments function and, particularly, how human beings can manage their behaviour and ecosystems in order to live sustainably. The term is often used to imply education within the school system, from primary to post-secondary. However, it is sometimes used more broadly to include all efforts to educate the public and other audiences, including print materials, websites, media campaigns etc. Related disciplines include outdoor education and experiential education. Environmental education is a learning process that increases people's knowledge and awareness about the environment and associated challenges, develops the necessary skills and expertise to address the challenges, and fosters attitudes, motivations, and commitments to make informed decisions and take responsible action

Environmental education has two components viz Environment and education. Education involves Knowledge, understanding and application of facts and concepts pertaining to a discipline and forming desirable believes, attitude, disposition, value as well as inculcation of interests pertaining to that discipline.

The purpose of environmental education is to improve the quality of environment, to create awareness among the people on environment problems and conservation. Therefore, the objectives of the environmental education are to generate awareness, Knowledge, attitude, Skills, evaluation ability and participation to help social groups and individuals.

FOCUSES OF ENVIRONMENTAL EDUCATION

1. Awareness and sensitivity about the environment and environmental challenges.
2. Knowledge and understanding about the environment and environmental challenges.
3. Attitude concern for the environment and help to maintain environmental quality.
4. Skills to mitigate the environmental problems.
5. Participation for exercising existing knowledge and environmental related programs.

ENVIRONMENTAL AWARENESS

"The Environment is everything that affects the individual except his genes". The term Environment refers to the surroundings of an organism, which includes both living and non living components. The components of Environment is viewed in different ways with different angles by different groups of people but it may be safely argued that environment is an inseparable whole and is constituted by the interacting systems of physical, biological and cultural elements which are interrelated individually as well as collectively in myriad ways.

The International Union for Conservation of Nature and Nature Resources defines Environmental Education as "the process of recognizing values and clarifying concepts in order to develop the skills and appreciate the interrelated among man, his culture and his biophysical surroundings".

Environmental awareness may be defined as to help the social groups and individuals to gain a variety of experience in and acquire a basic understanding of Environment and its associated problems. The concern of a small group of scientists and naturalists has become the focus of the society as a whole. Our survival depends both directly and indirectly upon the presence of stable eco-systems and stable cultivated eco-systems.

Environment Awareness is the ABC of Environmental Literacy Environmental Education Environmental Issues Environmental Programs and so on. It is the First step of the Ladder to Environmental Security for Sustainable development. Environment is closely linked to human beings and hence influences their health and quality of life. As such improving our environment by environmental awareness and education will improve human health and well being of all awareness.

Environmental education has been considered an additional or elective subject in much of traditional curriculum. At the elementary school level, environmental education can take the form of science enrichment curriculum, natural history field trips, community service projects, and participation in outdoor science schools. Environmental education policies assist schools and organizations in developing and improving environmental education programs that provide citizens with an in-depth understanding of the environment. School related Environmental education policies focus on three main components: curricula, green facilities, and training.

Schools can integrate environmental education into their curricula with sufficient funding from Environmental education policies. This approach is known as using the "environment as an integrating context" for learning inserts environmental education into the core subjects and thus environmental education does not take time away from other important subjects, such as art, gym, or music. In addition to finding environmental curricula in the classroom, environmental education policies allot the financial resources for hands-on, outdoor learning. These activities and lessons help address and mitigate "nature deficit disorder", as well as encourage healthier lifestyles.

Green schools, or green facility promotion, are another main component of environmental education policies. Greening school facilities cost, on average, a little less than 2 percent more than creating a traditional school, but payback from these energy efficient buildings occur within only a few years. Environmental education policies help reduce the relatively small burden of the initial start-up costs for green schools. Green school policies also provide grants for modernization, renovation, or repair of older school facilities. Additionally, healthy food options are also a central aspect of green schools. These policies specifically focus on bringing freshly prepared food, made from high-quality, locally grown ingredients into schools.

In secondary school, environmental curriculum can be a focused subject within the sciences or is a part of student interest groups or clubs. At the undergraduate and graduate level, it can be considered its own field within education, environmental studies, environmental science and policy, ecology, or human/cultural ecology programs.

Environmental education is not restricted to in-class lesson plans. There are numerous ways children can learn about the environment in which they live. From experiential lessons in the school yard and field trips to national parks to after-school green clubs and school wide sustainability projects, the environment is a topic which is readily and easily accessible. Furthermore, celebration of Earth Day or participation in EE week (run through the National Environmental Education Foundation) is a great way to dedicate your lessons to environmental education. To be most effective, promote a holistic approach and lead by example, using sustainable practices in the classroom and school grounds and encouraging students and parents to bring environmental education into their home.

The final aspect of environmental education policies, but certainly not least important, is training individuals to thrive in a sustainable society. In addition to building a strong relationship with nature, American citizens must have the skills and knowledge to succeed in a 21st century workforce. Thus, environmental education policies fund both teacher training and worker training initiatives. Teachers must be trained to effectively teach and incorporate environmental studies in their curricula. On the other hand, the current workforce must be trained or re-trained so that they can adapt to the new green economy. Environmental education policies that fund training programs are critical in educating citizens to prosper in a sustainable society.

RELATED DISCIPLINES

Environmental education has crossover with the disciplines of outdoor education and experiential education. Both disciplines complement environmental education yet have unique philosophies.

1. Outdoor education means learning "in" and "for" the outdoors. It is a means of curriculum extension and enrichment through outdoor experiences. Environmental education is often taught or enhanced through outdoor experiences. The out of doors experience, while not strictly environmental in nature, often contain elements of teaching about the environment.
2. Experiential education is a process through which a learner constructs knowledge, skill, and value from direct experiences experiential education can be viewed as both a process and method to deliver the ideas and skills associated with environmental education.

While each of these disciplines has their own objectives, there are points where both disciplines overlap with the intentions and philosophy of environmental education. Paraphrasing Webster collegiate Dictionary awareness implies vigilance in observing something or experience and alertness in drawing inferences from what one observes. Awareness in a personal development sense is a consciousness of which you are being and the impact that you are having on others. Heighten your awareness by imagining a small creature on your shoulder who watches over what you think and what you do and whispers what he observes in your ear.

The following guidelines should be considered to inculcate Environmental Education at school level

1. Environmental education at school level should aim at creating environmental awareness.
2. Environment concept should be integrated in existing courses in physical, natural and social sciences.

3. Students should be exposed to the concepts of nature education and the experience of participating in nature conservation programmes.
4. Various educational bodies should reorient early education curriculum to include environmental issues.
5. Extracurricular environmental programs for school children are a powerful tool for imparting environmental education to children and should be increasingly encouraged.
6. Several techniques for providing extracurricular environmental education to school children are available. These include sending out by mail by mail or distributing in the classroom entertaining children's magazines on environment, organization of nature and science clubs, visits to exhibitions and museums, organizing painting and essay competitions and exhibitions, participation in community environmental action program and using songs, plays folktales, puppet shows and environmental games and puzzles.
7. At the higher school level, it would be more purposeful to involve youth in seeking and finding solutions to environmental problems and thus indicate a positive environmental attitude.
8. Environmental magazines for the use of and teachers be brought out.
9. Periodical workshops and seminars on environmental topics should be arranged for teachers by organizations.
10. Besides text books, other kinds of teaching aids for environmental education such as guides, handbooks, slide shows, film models etc. should be developed.
11. Parent–Teachers associations should discuss environmental education strategies critically and evolve appropriate school-home integration for infusing the right attitude to environment in the children,
12. Program suited for non-school going and drop-out children should also be developed.

ENVIRONMENTAL EDUCATION AND AWARENESS

Public Education and awareness are the key factors in any attempt to maintain a proper balance and ensure sustainable development. Recognizing the potential of Environmental Education is an Effective instrument in preventing environmental crises and as an essential element of sustainable development Indian Environmental society has been engaged in spearheading Environmental Education and awareness from the very beginning. Indian Environmental society has undertaken a few new projects on environmental Education and is also continuing with some of the ongoing programs.

EDUCATION AND ENVIRONMENT

Environment influences one's education. The intersection between education and environment can be described as follows:

1. Education creates the urge for a clean environment.
2. It inculcates in the young minds the basic principles of sanitation and hygiene.
3. It helps pupils and students appreciate the need for conservation of our multifaceted heritage.
4. It teaches newer and environmentally safe technologies.

Environmental Education should start from the school level to pass on to Posterity our rich heritage. "The nation behaves well if it treats the natural resources as assets which it must turnover to the next generation increased and got impaired in Value"

OBJECTIVES FOR TEACHING ENVIRONMENTAL EDUCATION

The Belgrade charter has suggested the following

1. Awareness: To help individuals and social groups, acquire an awareness and sensitivity to the social environment and its associated problems.
2. Knowledge: To help individuals and social groups, acquire basic understanding of the total environment, its associated problems and humanity's critically responsible presence and role it.,
3. Attitude: To help individuals and social groups, acquire social values, strong feelings of concern for the environment and motivation to actively participate in its protection and improvement.
4. Skills: To help individuals and social groups, acquire the knowledge and skills of solving environmental problems.
5. Evaluation ability: To help individuals and social groups, evaluate environmental measure and educational programmes in term of ecological, political, economical, social, aesthetic and educational factors.
6. Participation: To help individuals and social groups, develop a sense of responsibility and urgency, regarding environmental problems to ensure appropriate action for solving the problems.

ENVIRONMENTAL EDUCATION CURRICULUM AND DIFFERENT APPROACHES

In order to achieve the objectives of the environmental education, the curriculum should be continuous, life-long and inter-disciplinary in its approach. The curriculum should be planned horizontally, embracing all the related subjects vertically dealing with one packing. The learners should receive insights into the environmental issues in the bio-physical, bio-chemical, bio-geological and bio-technological areas. The interdisciplinary approach may be in terms of drawing on the specific contents of each discipline in making possible a holistic and balance perspective. The Disciplines such as social sciences and environmental sciences should not be studied in isolation. The curriculum should be so flexible, that the material can be presented according to the background, needs and aspiration of the learners. It should be learner–oriented. They should create a learning environment, and assist learners as they search for information.

As the environmental education is concerned with man's life, it should include environment in its natural totality and built-up. In this connection, the environmental education should not be viewed as one or more subjects added to the already heavy-loaded into the curricular programs for all the learners, whatever be their age group and level of learning.

APPROACH FOR ENVIRONMENTAL EDUCATION

Newman (1981) described a 3-fold classification based on the disciplines.

1. **Environmental Studies:** This is concerned with the case of environmental disturbances and minimization of their import through social change (Social Sciences).
2. **Environmental Sciences:** This deals with the study of the processors in water, air, soil and organism, which lead to "pollution" or environmental damage and to find out a scientific basis for establishing a standard and healthy natural ecosystem.
3. **Environmental Engineering:** This deals with the study of the technical process, which can be used to minimize pollution and environmental impact. The objectives of environmental education are :
   - To improve the quality of environment.
   - To create an awareness among the people on environmental problems and conservation.
   - To develop skills to solve the environmental problems.
   - To create the necessary atmosphere to make it possible for citizens to participate in decision making and to develop the capabilities to evaluate the development programs.

PERSPECTIVE ON ENVIRONMENT EDUCATION

Environmental Education enhances public awareness and knowledge of environmental issues and challenges to civilization. Teachers are the backbone of a society. They play a crucial role in highlighting crucial environmental issues and implementing practical solutions to current local environmental problems in order to reduce the global environmental impact.

Environmental Education is a permanent process in which individuals gain awareness of their environment and acquire the knowledge, values, skills, experiences, and also the determination which will enable them to act individually and collectively to solve present and future environmental problems in order to meet their needs without compromising those of future generations.

Therefore, rather than defining a subject area, environmental education is a learning process featuring awareness of environment, acquiring knowledge, skills, values, experiences, and technical expertise to solve present and future environmental problems by acquiring holistic understanding of environmental problems. The Environmental Education may be summarized based on the following components:

- Earth is finite,
- All forms of life are important ,
- Everything is dynamic, interconnected and independent,
- Everything must go somewhere,
- Nature is not a gift from our forefathers but it is a loan from our grandchildren.

ENVIRONMENTAL ISSUES

Environmental education is vast and diverse by nature covering multidisciplinary areas. The principal goals of the teaching of Environmental Education are listed below:

- Helping people to develop a clear understanding about environment and its relationship with all human activities
- Understanding the concept of the inter relationship between natural, socioeconomic and political systems from the grassroots to the global levels as well as activities affecting the environment and major environment issues, such as pollution, occupational hazards, climate change, etc. The best example of it may be the global warming.
- Designing and running development and production processes from resources extraction to waste disposal in a holistic manner keeping understanding the need for incorporating environmental safeguards in industrial developmental projects and appreciating the need for obtaining environmental clearances.
- Developing the concept of Biodiversity.
- Developing Knowledge and skills for identifying and solving immediate local environmental problems, and maintaining on eco-friendly work environment.

- Understanding the concept of stewardship and motivation critical thinking, reflection and decision making that is reflected in personal life styles.

AWARENESS OF THE SCHOOL STUDENTS BY THE USE OF VARIOUS MODELS OF TEACHING

Emergence of environmental education as a compulsory component of curriculum at school level is a welcome step. India, a developing country, can restore environmental and natural processes by proper awareness on such issues among its citizens. It is a new field and not much canvassing is being done by the public media. Teaching of environmental education is the most burning problem of the country; for this the role of the teacher and his by /her methodology of teaching crucial. Teachers quantum of Knowledge and understanding of Environment is directly related with the objectives and problem of Environmental Education. Since the need of hour is environmentally oriented citizens, the teachers being the national builders have the responsibility to produce such conscious citizens. If we want secure the future of Environment; we have to create awareness about the environment and an attitude for caring and sharing of natural resource among children who are the feature citizen of our nation as rightly said by Pandit Jawaharlal Nehru, The first prime minister of Independent India that "feature of India is shaped in her class rooms" where students are the foundations and teachers are the pillars of development.

One important purpose of education is to provide an understanding of the world environment from physical, biological, social, economical, and political point of view. This understanding also requires the study of the in numerable problems which the man kind faces today. An understanding of environmental problems can be developed by first creating awareness than developing appropriate solution for the Environment. These problems have resulted in a global effort to include aspects of Environmental Education in school curriculum at all levels in on appropriate manner. However, the objective of Environmental Education cannot be realized simply by infusing Environmental concept into the existing curriculum. The effective infusing of Environmental Education curriculum into school programs is possible only when teachers possess the knowledge, and skills and effective attributes which they will impart to the students. The Teachers should use proper methods to transfer Knowledge skills to pupils.

In spite of International efforts, the progress of Environmental Education in world scene does not present a very satisfying picture. It seems that Environmental education has been more accepted than actuated particularly in developing countries.

Environmental Activity

Environmental Activity was done by the students to have direct experience of the Environment in the real life under the supervising of teacher.

Educational Implications

Environment Education is broad based and is strongly related with basic principles of general Education. The various models of teaching Environmental Education have been useful improving the quality of Education through different subject in different classes especially at higher secondary level. Environmental education helps to produce citizens who are environmentally knowledgeable skilled. It leads them towards maintaining a dynamic equilibrium between quality of life and the quality of the Environment.

NEED FOR THE STUDY

Human beings have always exploited the resources available in their natural surroundings for their benefit. Air, Water, land, the Atmosphere living organisms – each of these elements is of important in some form or other to human beings. However technological advancement has made human beings rapacious in their exploitation of natural resources.

India faces environmental challenges on two fronts: Poverty as well as economic development. Poverty and Population pressure clearly result in overuse of land, water forests and other resources without thought of future for who wants to think of coming generations when it is so difficult to survive today? Uncontrolled economic development overuse of groundwater systems and population of natural resources has become the order of the day. So it is the need of the hour to implement Environmental education in full swing. Education is the only way to Environmental Awareness.

It is to effectively educate man regarding his relationship to the total environment the relationship which based on the mutually of respect rather than on superior subordinate relationship. Hence major goals of environmental education should be to help individuals acquire:

1. A Clear understanding that man is an in separable part of the biosphere which consists of man and his built in environment the excising bio physical environment and the substances of the ecological balance. The basic responsibility of the society and government to work for solving environmental problems.
2. Development of Environmental ethics which will motivate people to participate in the decision making process and to demand protection of the environment so as to advance human welfare and dignity.

3. Environmental Education should aim to provide factual information to students which will lead to the understanding of the intricate system of ecological balance and man's place in it. To foster Environmental Education awareness is one of the main factors of awareness and concern about economic, social, political and ecological interdependence in urban and rural areas. Tuticorin Educational District is situated in the southern coast of Tamil Nadu. It is an Industrial area. This induced the investigator to make an attempt to study the awareness on environmental education among the Higher Secondary Students at Salem Educational District.

OBJECTIVES OF THE STUDY

The Following Objectives were formulated for the present Study.To find out the environmental awareness of higher secondary school students in Salem Educational District.

To find out the significant difference in the environmental awareness of

1. Gender
2. Student Locality
3. Types of school
4. Parent occupation
5. School locality

STATEMENT OF THE PROBLEM

Environmental Awareness is necessary to know the importance of keeping the environment clean and protecting the earth. So the study focuses on the topic entitled ***"A Study on Environmental Awareness of Standard XI Students in Salem District".***

HYPOTHESES OF THE STUDY

1. There is no significant difference between aided boys & Aided girls towards awareness on environmental education among Higher Secondary students at Salem District.
2. There is no significant difference between boys and girls towards awareness on environmental education among Higher Secondary Students at Salem District.
3. There is no significant difference between rural and urban students towards awareness on environmental education among Higher Secondary students at Salem District.
4. There is no significant difference between rural and urban schools towards awareness on environmental education among Higher Secondary students at Salem District.

5. There is no significant difference between Government and Private Parents Occupation towards awareness on environmental education among Higher Secondary students at Salem District.
6. There is no significant difference between Government Boys and girls towards awareness on environmental education among Higher Secondary students at Salem District.

SCOPE OF ENVIRONMENTAL STUDIES

Environmental Study is an important tool to educate the people for preserving quality environment. The main scope of environmental studies includes.

1. To get an awareness and sensitivity to the total environment and its related problems.
2. To motivate the active participation in environmental protection and Improvement.
3. To develop skills for identifying and solving environmental problems.
4. To know the necessity of conservation of natural resources.
5. To Evaluate Environmental Programs in terms of social economic ecological and aesthetic factors

ABOUT HIGHER SECONDARY STUDENTS

After the Completion of the High School level of education students enter the secondary level i.e. in Standard XI in Higher Secondary School. Now they attain the adolescence stage as teenagers.

SALEM DISTRICT

Since Salem is a growing industrialized town it is apt for the study and also special for steel and the mango.

DELIMITATION OF THE STUDY

1. The study has been limited to Salem District only.
2. The study has been restricted to the Higher Secondary students only.
3. This study adopted survey method using questionnaires to collect data from respondents.
4. A purposive stratified random sample was used to choose the subject to be included in the study.
5. This study is focused mainly on the variables, gender, and student's locality, types of the school, parents occupation, and school locality.

ORGANIZATION OF THE THESIS:

- The first chapter gives introduction, definitions of the terms, statement of problem, objectives and limitation of the study.
- Second chapter deals with the review of related literature which are done in India and abroad related to this problem.
- Third chapter gives a detailed account of research procedures and methodology used in this problem.
- Fourth chapter deals with the tabulation of analysis and the interpretation of the data in detail.
- Fifth chapter describes the findings, conclusion and certain recommendations about the problem.

❐

12

Review of Related Literature

"A good thesis is one that me how to replicate or extend the previous work with improvements to reduce bias, eliminate flaws consider pertinent variables, settle unsolved issues to check contradictory or uncertain finding".

The aim of this chapter is to record briefly a survey of literature related to the problems under study. It is necessary to enter on any research project. This will help in understanding the various aspects of the problem.

The research worker must be acquainted with up-to-date information about what has been thought and done in the specific area from which he intends to take up a problem of research.

A review of related literature gives the scholar an understanding of the previous work that has been done in the area, it enables him to know the means of getting to the frontier in the field of his problems, methods and limitations and it enables him to locate comparative data useful in the interpretation of results.

REVIEW OF RELATED LITERATURE

A review of related literature is a direction of find out the reality and the beneficial nature and the reliability of a work undertaken, keeping in mind the material that are available in connection with the topic. A review will give the investigator a vivid idea of what he should do and how he should go about his investigation. Clarke, D.H and Clarke, H.H. (1970) gave the importance of review of related literature as that of before completing a plan for a research understanding, the investigator needs to conduct a literature search in the area of the proposed investigations.

The review of related literature is an instrument in the selection of the topic formulation of hypothesis and defective reasoning leading to the problem. It helps to get a clear idea and supports the findings with regard to the problem under study (Tirumalai Swamy1995).

The research scholar had come across several books, periodicals, journals, internet and unpublished thesis while searching for relevant facts and findings that are related to this present study. Such of these facts are given below for a better understanding and to justify his study.

PURPOSE OF REVIEW LITERATURE

The phrase Review of literature consists of two words Review and Literature of a particular are of any discipline which includes theoretical practical and its research studies.

The literature in any field forms the foundation upon which all future work will be build. If we fail to build foundations of knowledge provided by the review of literature one work is likely to be shadow and that has already done better by someone else.

A search for knowledge cannot yield something meaningful if this relation with the existing knowledge has not been examined. A research study is never conducted in a vacuum. Hence an attempt was made, as far as possible, to find out what has already been done. A review of literature gives both thematic as well as methodological direction. In a rare case a study may justify accomplishment of a new knowledge without paying attention to what has been done carrier. In an age where we already find vast store of knowledge, it is necessary to examine what has been done before we boast of a new achievement (Barotia and Sharma, 1999). Hence, a brief review of the studies related to the present problem is described in this chapter.

The following are the some of the purposes of the review of literature.

1. It provides ideas, theories, explanations or hypothesis valuable in formulation the problem.
2. To avoid the risk of duplicating some of the studies already undertaken.
3. To suggest methods or research methodology appropriate to the problem.
4. It suggests valuable basis for hypothesis.
5. It helps delimit the problem.
6. It helps the investigator not to allow the mistake (or) pit fall which occurred in the previous findings.

7. To locate comparative data useful in the interpretation of results.
8. It contributes to the investigator for the general scholarship.
9. studies conducted in India

Arundhati Vishvasrao, Various ideas have been introduced for teaching environmental sciences through formal education. These attempts have created environmental awareness, but Environmental Education has still not been achieved. For bridging the gap between environmental awareness and education three important changes are proposed:

1. The focus of science education must change from creationism to a naturalistic view, right from school.
2. The learner must remain the focus and must develop a holistic understanding of his environment.
3. Environment friendly habits must be developed from school days, wherein teachers become role models in the formal education system.

Awareness leads to understanding and understanding to action. Awareness leads to information', which develops an understanding of the 'science' and leads to action, which is culture (ethics). Ancient Indian culture allowed the population to put environmental ethics into practice. This was achieved through role models. The Gurukul system practiced in India at that time is a very good example of this.

Ehsan [1985] examined the nature and scope of the environmental studies programs in the primary schools of Bangladesh in terms of their objectives, content and teaching learning strategies his findings were treat

1. The objectives of teaching environmental science were not explicitly stated in the program
2. The contents of topics included in the programme were up-to-date and suitable to learner's needs ,interests and abilities
3. The teaching learning strategies suggested in the programme were feasible and practicable for use by teachers in the class-room.

Guptha [1986] in his study attempted to develop a tool which can measure the attitude of teachers towards environmental education the data for his study were collected from150 teachers working in primary and secondary schools and junior colleges. The study showed that the teachers had favourable attitude towards environmental education. But the degree of favourableness was the highest among .college teachers .the study identified that crowded class room's lack of time for proper planning of activities and loss of interest in the absence of follow up actions as stumbling blocks to the implementation of environmental education program.

Rath N.C. Mohanthy [1992] jointly conducted a study to assess the awareness of adolescents on Environmental pollution.

1. It was found that 59 percent of the school going adolescents had medium level of awareness while19 percent and 22 percent of them had high and low level of awareness on environmental pollution, respectively. Among the non school adolescents, it was observed that 68 percent of them had medium level of awareness while 17percent and15percent of them had high and low level of Awareness on environmental pollution respectively.
2. It was presumed that education has got definite impact on the awareness of environmental pollution. The more an individual becomes educated, the higher will be his or her awareness on environmental pollution.
3. It was revealed that out of the total respondents 1153 and 36 percent were having low, high medium exposure, to media respectively. The 'r' value indicated exposure, to different media and the .awareness towards environmental pollution only in the case of school going, adolescents. In the case of nonschool going adolescents .also, the relationship between exposure to media and awareness existed but it was weak and statistically in significant.

Reddy [1992] studied the use of environ mental mode in teaching primary classes the study revealed that the use of environment was effective in teaching. By making effective use of this device pupils can be helped to become active learners. It creates class room more interesting and attracts the pupils to come to schools .It improves the enrolment reduces dropouts. Thus use of environment helps in achieving universalization of elementary education.

According to singh and singh [1992] environmental education is an investment in future the environmental education in children is likely to result in greater consciousness about global issues, an improved healthful loving and greater prosperity due to more judicious use of natural resources. Environmental education creates personal commitment to, or acceptance of responsibility for the proper maintenance of the environment. Benefits from the environmental education will always be positive whatever be the expenditure involved

Swatantra Devi [1992] identified a few strategies for the teaching of environmental education. She suggested a few activities to facilitate teaching and learning process of environmental knowledge to secondary school students. She suggested that problem solving Approach, use of visual aids and follow up in terms of class discussions were effective strategies. She delineated the benefits and risks involved in sticking to single strategy.

Sundararajan.S and Rajashekar.S [1993] conducted a study on "Environmental awareness among higher secondary students. The study revealed that the environmental awareness of the higher secondary students in Tamil Nadu had not been influenced by the locality to which they belong or by their sex .similarly no significant difference existed between student's environmental awareness and there, socio-economic, background or their special subject of study .

V.M. Galushin [1994] noted that there are three kinds of approaches to school environmental education.

1. Environmental topics may is dispersed throughout the entire curriculum by insertions at appropriate places in the syllabi of various, disciplines.
2. A specially designed lesson on nature, conservancy may be inserted as a unit, within the framework, of one of the existing school subjects.
3. An integrated course of environmental education may be offered as a separate discipline on par with other school subjects.
4. He felt that three approaches may be used in successive stages, rather than as alternatives.

Irmeli Palmberg [2000] Mostly students describe Environmental issues as increasing problems and horrible disasters as presented in mass media. Only a small minority of students has more optimistic views and trust in time, changes in man's environmental attitude and lifestyle for they simply put their trust in new technology.

K. Durga Malathi [2002] found that there is a significant difference between rural and urban regions and gender difference in the environmental awareness.

G.C.Pradhan [2002] show that the teachers teaching science had significantly higher awareness compared to teachers of social science and languages.

M. Selvam, G. Anto Boopalrajan, B. William Dharma Raja [2003] another study revealed that teacher trainees had significant difference in terms of age.

Joanne[2004] A study suggested combining Environmental Education and artwork in the primary grade for sustainability day.

M.Balamurugan [2005] Association could be seen between environmental awareness and fathers' occupations as skilled workers. Some findings showed significant difference in environmental awareness, and religious groups and school types.

P.Dharani[2005] A study on student's perception on 'Disaster Management' found that there is a correlation of perception of school students between the natural and manmade disaster management.

Fishman, Lianne [2005] Some international investigations revealed promoting of opportunities for children to experience nature first hand on the way to school, the promotion of children's awareness of nature in their daily lives and the promotion of interest and tolerance of local plants and animals .

Mercy Abraham, Arjunan NK [2005] another study found that there is no significant difference between girls and boys in secondary classes with record to their pre-environmental.

R.Sahaya mary, I. Paul Raj [2005] Studies showed that boys especially from urban area have more awareness than girls. Some studies revealed that science students have more awareness of biodiversity and conservation than non-science students.

Sandhya Gihar [2006] Finding of another study revealed that male students and scientific background students were having higher environmental responsibility behavior than their counterparts.

Ami Mat & Yahaya, Nurizon & Ahmadun, Fakhrul-Razi [2007] Findings show that environmental awareness had raised the consciousness of students but was rather im effective in changing action and behavior patterns.

Dr. R. Gnanadevan [2007] Findings revealed that environmental awareness of Hr. Sec students is high.

Shobeiri, S.M., Omidvar B and Prahallada N.N [2007] A comparative study revealed that there are significant differences in Indian and Iranian students in their environmental Awareness.

Chandrasekar [2008] from the review of journals, it could be observed that some investigation had been conducted to find out the level of environmental awareness among tenth standard high school students of Hyderabad city. Findings concluded that environmental awareness of high school students is moderate.

An analysis of level of environmental awareness: the case of prospective teachers (2010) G.Ekambaram, B.Nagaraja In this study, the investigators among other things found that the level of environmental awareness differs among science and non-science teachers with science teachers having a higher level of environmental awareness.

Objectives of the study were

Though the study in general aims at an analysis of awareness among under-training teachers, it specifically aims at the following objectives:

1. To analyze the levels of awareness about environment among prospective teachers.
2. To compare and contrast the attitude of science and non-science prospective teacher with regard to environmental awareness, and
3. To evaluate the impact of gender, age and social status of the prospective teachers on the level of environmental awareness.

Sample Size

Keeping the objectives in view, a total of 200 prospective teachers, who are under B Entraining in Tirupati College were selected at random, consisting of 112 Science trainee-teachers and 88 non-science trainee teachers in Chittoor district of Andhra Pradesh.

Summary of Findings

The analysis of level of awareness of 200 sample prospective teachers consisting of Science and Non-Science, male and female, different age groups and social groups indicate that;

1. The level of awareness differs in Science and Non-Science teachers. Science teachers were found with higher level of environmental awareness compared to Non-Science teachers.
2. Gender difference also was found in the level of awareness. The results of the analysis show that level of environmental awareness was higher among female sample teachers compared to male sample teachers.
3. An exercise is also made to know the impact of some selected social variables like age and social status. The age-wise analysis of the level of awareness reveals that there is statistically significant difference in the sample teachers who are in the age groups of below 23 years and above 23 years.
4. The social status wise analysis of the level of awareness revealed that there is statically significant difference in the level of awareness between the sample teacher representing other classes and SC and ST social group. The sample teachers belonging to other classes had higher level of awareness compared to SC and ST teachers.
5. No statistically significant difference was found in the level of awareness between the sample teachers belonging to backward classes and others forward classes and also between backward classes and scheduled caste and schedule tribes.
   Studies conducted in ABROAD

Madduma Bandara C.M. [1989] examines the need to increase awareness of the interactions between human activity and environmental change based on the HDGC (Human Dimension of Global Change Programme) perspective. In addition to that, the whole issue is referred to various international conferences regarding the impacts global environmental education has on the poorest and weaker groups in developing countries. This reading also talks about the target groups for these educational initiatives but also notes what he calls "a continuing need to reach out to the unconverted groups in most developing Countries".

Although international environmental education has a global perspective, the author identifies "special" target groups with special problems. Mainly populations in rural areas form these groups. Most people in these zones are among the poorest and most ill educated on the plane. They are subject to numerous factors that don't facilitate the implementation of sustainable management plans, factors that relate to simple survival needs, which are more important to their lives than environmental concerns.

Environmental awareness in vulnerable communities in developing countries can be improved through both formal and non-formal education. Mass media, art, and traditional knowledge, are elements that can greatly contribute to the encouragement of environmental awareness in developing countries.

Filho [1995] also notes that in the relatively short history of "the environment" as a social problem, public concern has been cyclical and so has the media coverage of environmental news.

Leal Filho [1995] declares; "to ensure didactic potential of the media for environmental information and for environmental education is fully used, there are a number of items, which need to be considered. Some of these are:

1. Diversity of information: newspaper articles, as well as television and radio programs may be used as resource materials for classroom-based lessons provided that due guidance is given and that the issues discussed may be closely related to curricular themes.
2. Time relevance: the use of printed or broadcast materials ought to provide a supply of recent information with up-to-date details.
3. Accuracy: Teachers and others using the media for environmental education should be aware of this reality and try to carefully select materials prior to use, so that misunderstanding and misinformation may be prevented."

Tilbury [1995] argues that Environmental Education for Sustainability differs from previous environmental Education approaches in that it focuses more sharply on developing closer links between environmental quality, ecology and socio-economic and the political threads which underlie it. Its basis is the creation of a more holistic outlook on problems, requiring a deeper integration between the study of environment and development problems.

Although there is a great deal of work required to develop meaningful and workable definitions of Environmental Education for Sustainability, the following elements are important:

1. Ethical awareness
2. Shaping values and attitudes
3. Skills and behaviour consistent with sustainable development

4. Effective public participation in decision making
5. Making decisions and taking action
6. Consideration of future generations.

Of the indicators used in the mapping process, a sub-set of 36 specifically pertaining to environmental education for sustainability were also used to further evaluate and rate course content in relation to the above elements.

As Smyth [1995] Environmental education is a cross curriculum topic promoting global awareness, sustainable living and active citizenship. It involves a structured and planned process that seeks the implementation of environmental curriculum at educational institutions at different levels. Cross-cutting subjects that are integrated in a global perspective but that can be learned and applied locally should implement this curriculum.

Based on these principles we might assert that Environmental education should be multilevel and continuous. A first educational level should target special programs for non-formal adult and community-based audiences. The second level focuses on secondary school. It involves teaching the main disciplines within an environmental context. The third level focuses on obtaining environment based professional skills within the different professional disciplines. An urgent need to educate humankind on conservation and sustainable uses of natural resources through environmental education has been accepted as a global necessity. The concept of environmental education gained great momentum at the UN conference in Stockholm in 1972. In

Agenda 21 a holistic view of Environmental education was adopted and acknowledged by 175 countries at the first UN Earth summit in Rio de Janeiro on environment and development. The now famous "Agenda 21" identifies education as a vital aid to support all the needed changes for sustainability to take place. Signatory nations agreed to pursue actions to include environment sustainable development as a cross cutting matter in curriculum at different levels of education, and also to ensure it reaches different audiences, including those located at remote communities .

As Smyth (1995) lays it out, "Agenda 21 signals the need for a clear lead from the top and for facilitation of collaboration between the main interests concerned, in national and local government, government agencies, formal education, the business sector, cultural, community and youth organizations and the voluntary sector. All of these are concerned in different ways with direct educational activity and services, whether formal or informal, with staff training and with exemplary environmental practice and there is an often unrealized potential for collaborative programs."

The main goal of Agenda 21 is that all signatory countries incorporate Environmental education into their educational systems at all levels. Norway and Malta represent two examples of countries that are trying to implement environmental curricula in their educational systems. They have both experienced difficulties but they have also made progress. Their efforts deserve analysis because they demonstrate many positive aspects that can be applied elsewhere if locally adapted.

It is obvious there is a need to tackle environmental problems globally by means of a systematic process that requires changes in traditional education schemes. The entire scientific community is reasonably responsible for getting involved in adequate public relations efforts that enable communication of its research, concerns and uncertainties, to the institutions, organizations and governing bodies responsible for education. Similarly establishments responsible for education should make efforts that direct to the public information received from scientists in effective and understandable ways.

As Pace notes [1997], elementary school curricula are essentially fragmented and mono-disciplinary, making interdisciplinary learning hard to apply. Even though environmental topics have become much more relevant in recent years in secondary schools, it is also fragmentary.

While environmental education is not a national Maltese priority, at least there is a growing awareness phase by government and other organizations where the need to incorporate environmental topics into their educational system is being recognized. Different organizations have included environmental education in their agendas. However, they have been forced to work in an uncoordinated way due mainly to a lack of official support and organization.

As Pace (1997) declares, "In an attempt to improve the situation the Education Division, the Environment Secretariat, the faculty of education and some nongovernmental organizations jointly organized the Second National Training Workshop on Environmental Education in Malta (May 1995). The goal of the event was that of getting all those involved in environmental education together to; become aware of the state of environmental education in the region, identify the problems, needs and support required for the successful implementation of environmental education initiatives and, to discuss the possibility of coordinating these initiatives so as to improve their effectiveness".

While Malta has a long way to go before a national environmental education strategy can be fully implemented in their educational system, the country has at least recognized the intention of incorporating environmental education into their education system and some efforts in this direction are being produced.

Benedict [1999] points out "The goal of the Ministry of Education's strategy was that all pupils should receive environmental education in line with the UNESCO goals, including knowledge, attitudes, capabilities and behaviour.

A rather large group of teachers, researchers and organizations was involved in developing the strategy, which went through several stages of revision and is still being periodically revised. Thus, the Ministry of Education itself has taken a leading role in initiating change. Staffing (one full-time position) and a substantial budget were allocated to this work, which was led by the Ministry of Education."

According to Benedict's study (1999) the goals of the Norwegian strategy were oriented toward the system as a whole, not individual schools or programs.

Goals

1. Clarify the goals and contents of environmental education.
2. Contribute to organizational development in schools.
3. Ensure that the strategy is implemented.
4. Clarify and coordinate efforts in environmental education between the school system and its cooperative partners.

Evaluation

These goals touch on three of the four 'Cs': commitment and responsibility, and on the part of the Ministry of Education, competence and cooperation. Curriculum was being dealt with in a general curriculum reform so it did not appear in the strategy goals.

According to Benedict (1999) the most important lessons learned from the Norwegian case are, "First, shortcuts don't work. Teachers who struggle to implement systemic environmental education within the framework of an educational system that isn't made for it may succeed in the classroom in the short term, but their efforts are usually not sustainable. Teachers cannot succeed without support from the higher levels and the Ministry of Education cannot do well in conducting educational development without full cooperation from teachers and principals.

A second is that the process of bringing about systemic changes in priorities, competence, curricula and patterns of cooperation and communication is a long term process. Experiences in Norway indicate that raising teacher's competence in environmental education will require much more than short in-service training courses, although these kinds of courses can be effective in initial awareness rising. Understanding the cross-cutting elements between natural and human systems is intellectually challenging and requires openness to a wide range of disciplinary paradigms, from history, anthropology and literature to economics, biology and political science.

A third is that structural changes in communication and cooperation require patience, goodwill and commitment. Vertical communication between the Ministry of Education and local bodies such as municipal school directors and schools is full of tensions. Some sort of compromise by both parts and understanding of the roles and responsibilities must be reached if change is to be possible."

Cooperation between the Ministry of Education and Ministry of the Environment in Norway is also a sensitive subject. They can easily step on the other's "territory" and put at risk vital mutual aid. Cooperation and network building between the school and external players is fundamental to efficient environmental education.

As Allen [2001] says; "Scientists and journalists have had plenty of positive interactions. Yet despite the idealistic motivations of scientists and professional journalists, chaos and hard feelings sometimes characterize the interactions between them. Such discord is largely the result of a clash of two cultures, science and the newsroom. Framed simply, science is the world of labs, publications, peer review, and acceptance according to the values and norms of science. Journalism's task is to inform the public speedily, to detail history on the run."

Nkosi [2002] carried out a community oriented education program on biological diversity, conservation and sustainability in Swaziland. It emphasized the need for a public education program. This program was intended to be seen as an investment in the people by teaching them a self-regulating culture that would help raise awareness of the role biodiversity and conservation can play in sustainable development among the most vulnerable communities in the developing world.

De Lorme et al. [2003] reviewed the connection between human growth, development and water resources in central Florida. By including six focal groups, the report was based on the importance input from the community had in contributing to the preproduction stages of a public educational campaign in the region. The groups recommended five messages and five key delivery options that could be included in the campaign.

Messages

1. Make clear to homeowners the financial advantages of long-term water management practices.
2. Promote self-efficacy at home.
3. Make evident the association between quality of water and quality of life.
4. Recognize the demographic characteristics of the region.
5. Keep the messages straightforward and brief.

Delivery

1. Water resource information could be delivered through direct mail in utility bills.
2. Messages could be delivered through public service announcements and stories on local television programs.
3. The use of websites and electronic newsletters can be positive.
4. Messages and information could be distributed through educational programs in the school system where parents are able to participate.
5. Information kits could be delivered through homeowner's associations.

Vaughan [2003], Environmental education and community conservation needs should be viewed in a continuous and progressive perspective. A study conducted during a 4-week period in the town of Quebrada Ganado, Costa Rica by Vaughan revealed that if Environmental Education programs for children are guided in a proper way, parents and other adults could also benefit from them. Knowledge gain passed on from children to parents (and other adults) indicates that awareness can be delivered in a consecutive way from the classroom to the community

ANALOGY

Out of total thirty four studies identified, the investigator found twenty three studies conducted in India and eleven studies conducted in abroad. Majority of the studies belongs to survey studies and few of them are experimental studies.

Most of the studies followed random sampling technique in the collection of data and the size of the selected samples range from to samples. In majority of the studies the questionnaire, Opionnarrie rating scale developed by the investigator was utilized as a tool. Since all the reviewed studies were related to awareness on Environmental Education. In majority of the studies of the data was collected only from the school students and no standardized tool was catalyzed. Mean, standard deviation and 't' test were the statistical technique followed in the majority of the study.

Durga Malathi K.[2002] states that there is a significant difference between rural and urban regions and gender difference in the environmental awareness. This finding is related to the present study.

Ehsan [1985], Sundararajan.S and Rajashekar.S [1993], GalushinV.M. [1994], Pradhan G.C. [2002], Dr. R. Gnanadevan [2007] states that states about environmental education. This finding is related to the present study.

The following chapter deals with the methodology of the present study.

13

Methodology of the Study

OVERVIEW

The Methodology followed in the present study is described in this Chapter. The present study is a Normative Survey Research which aimed to measures the Awareness on Environmental Education among Higher Secondary Students. The Design of the study, construction of the Tool, Pilot Study, Validity and Reliability, Size of the Sample, Selection of the Sample, Administering the Tool among the Students, Scoring Methods, Statistical Techniques utilized etc., have been reported in detailed manner in this present Chapter and ends with the Limitations of the study.

DESIGN OF THE STUDY

Research design is a plan, a structure and a strategy of investigation conceived to obtain answers to various issues in research. The object of research design is to test the research hypotheses. The research design, therefore, is built in the principle of maximization of the results of the study, minimization of variance. A research design however, is not a highly specific plan to be followed without direction. Rather, it is series of guideposts to keep right direction. Thus, research design is the process of planning a research, choosing methods and procedures that can be expected to yield meaningful and most interpretable results.

TABLE.13.1: Schematic Representation of the Research Design

S.No	Type	Sources
1.	Nature of the research	Normative Survey Research
2.	Tools Developed	Awareness on Environmental Education among Higher Secondary Students(AEEHSS)
3.	Variables	Students
4.	Demographic Variables	• Gender • Student's Locality • Types of School • Parent Occupation • School Locality
5.	Sampling Technique	Stratified Random Sampling Technique.
6.	Size of the Sample	Students – 150 Boys -72 Girls-78
7.	Statistical Techniques used	Mean, Standard Deviation, 't' test

The present study belongs to Normative Survey Research. In this, Demographic Variables like Gender, Students Locality, Types of School, Parent Occupation and School Locality are used. The Tool use in the Study is Awareness on Environmental Education among Higher Secondary Students at Salem District, along with a Personal Data Sheet to know the background of the Students; Random Sampling technique was followed in this study. Data were collected from 150 Students in different locations of Salem District. The Statistical Techniques were used Mean, S.D and 't' Test.

OBJECTIVE OF THE STUDY

1. To find out the level of significant different between Aided boys and Aided girls towards awareness on Environmental education among Higher Secondary students at Salem district.
2. To find out the level of significant different between boys and girls towards awareness on Environmental education among Higher Secondary students at Salem district.
3. To find out the level of significant different between rural and urban students towards awareness on Environmental education among Higher Secondary students at Salem district.
4. To find out the level of significant different between rural and urban school's towards awareness on Environmental education among Higher Secondary students at Salem district.

5. To find out the level of significant different government and private parents occupation towards awareness on Environmental education among Higher Secondary students at Salem district.
6. To find out the level of significant different government boys and government girls towards awareness on Environmental education among Higher Secondary students at Salem district.

HYPOTHESES OF THE STUDY

1. There is no significant difference between aided boys & Aided girls towards awareness on environmental education among Higher Secondary students at Salem District.
2. There is no significant difference between boys and girls towards awareness on environmental education among Higher Secondary Students at Salem District.
3. There is no significant difference between rural and urban students towards awareness on environmental education among Higher Secondary students at Salem District.
4. There is no significant difference between rural and urban schools towards awareness on environmental education among Higher Secondary students at Salem District.
5. There is no significant difference between Government and Private Parents Occupation towards awareness on environmental education among Higher Secondary students at Salem District.
6. There is no significant difference between Government Boys and girls towards awareness on environmental education among Higher Secondary students at Salem District.

TOOL USED FOR THE STUDY

To access the awareness on Environmental Education among Higher Secondary Students in Salem District with three types of Four Point Rating Scale was developed under the objective of the study. In the type of tool, with the options such as Strongly Agree, Agree, Disagree and Strongly Disagree were utilized.

PRELIMINARY DRAFT OF THE TOOL

The investigator being a Teacher Educator was going on to write appropriate statements related to the objectives of the study and reflect the aim of the study. The steps on the different issues based on the experience of Teachers and other aspects the investigator refine the written statements in all the Opinonnairre. After the corrections, the Opinonnairre had 50 Statements only. Then it was administered as a Pilot Study.

PILOT STUDY

The above Opinonnairre was neatly typed and administered among the 40 Students, their respective our College Staffs and our College B.Ed Students in the time of Pilot Study the two Opinonnairre had 50 statements for students. After completion of the pilot study, gathered valuable suggestions, corrections and deleting of some statements were taken by the investigator and refine the Opinonnairre. Finally the tool AEEHSS was consists of 50 statements, the above the tools were used to a study on finding the Awareness on Environmental Education among Higher secondary Students at Salem District.

TABLE.13.2: Distribution of Positive and Negative Statements of Asebs

S.No	Students		Total
	Positive Items	**Negative Items**	
1.	1,3,5,6,8,9,10,12,15,18,19,21,22,24,25,26,28,29,30,32,34,37,39,40,42,43,45,46,50.	2,4,7,11,13,14,16,17,20,23,27,31,33,35,36, 38,41,44,48,49	
	30	20	50

The above table 13.2 shows the student Opinonnairre to access the students awareness on Environmental education this tool AEEHSS consists of 4 point scale with 30 positive and 20 negative statements.

Reliability

A reliable scale agrees with itself and measure consistently that which it is supposed to measure. The same yard stick applied to the same individual or subject should yield the same value from moment to the moment, provided the thing measured has itself not changed.

The reliability of a scale may be determined in four different ways.

1. The test-retest method
2. Alternate or parallel from method
3. The spilt half method
4. National equivalence

The spilt half method is regarded as the best of the methods. The main advantages in this method is the fact of that data for calculating reliability are got upon one instance, so that the variations brought about by differences between the two testing situations are eliminated considering these the investigator preferred this method for computing reliability.

The useful procedure is to spilt the whole list into two halves, odd numbered illustrated in the table 5, taking two groups one along the 'x' axis the other along the 'y' axis. The pear son's product moment correlation was calculated by using the formula in this simplest form.

Form the reliability of the half test, the self correlation of the to hole test was calculated using the spearmen brown prophecy formula where r testing is the reliability co efficient of the whole test and r is the reliability co efficient of the test. In this case the value of r'=0.71 and applying the prophecy formula r=0.86. this is highly significant.

Validity

The problem of insuring validity in attitude scales is a particularly difficult one because attitudes can be measured only indirectly. Techniques for determining validity are ill-developed and poorly standardized.

A valid scale should be reliable also. But a reliable scale need not necessarily be valid. A valid scale measures that which it is supported to measure. Three methods are ordinarily used to test the validity of attitude scales. They are:

1. Logical test of validity-a scale is said to be valid if it does not violate any accepted theory by its measurement.
2. Pragmatic test-if the scores of the scale confirmed common sense observation and experience the scale is declared valid.
3. The verbal responses can be checked with has verbal behavior towards a particular thing or issue. The scores of the scale are correlated with one or more independent criteria of phenomena being measured.

Types of Validity

Broadly, five types of validity are discussed in the literature on testing. They are:

1. Content validity
2. Criterion-related validity
   - Con-current.
   - Predictive.
3. Construct validity.
4. Face validity.
5. Factorial validity.

Content validity

Content validity also means logical or curricular activity. Content validity is best considered in relation to achievement test. 'An Achievement test has content represents faithfully the objectives of a given instructional sequence and reflects the emphasis accorded to these objectives as the instruction was carried out thus, the content validity is determined by the fact that it adequately coves both the content and objectives of the subject matters unit on which the test is based. The test, in this sense, gives equal weight age to all the aspects'. The overall extent of agreement between the test and the instructional plan.

Prof. Lindeman sounds a point of warning. He says that 'an achievement test may have adequate content validity at a given time for a particular class and teacher but may not be equally valid for testing another group taught by a different teacher at a different time'. So, he suggests, "one should, however, keep in mind that the content validity of a test is not necessarily a fixed and changeless characteristics. It must be examined a new whenever the test is used with a different group or when the testing situation is altered".

Construct validity

Construct validity of a test refers to the extent to which the test measures a particular characteristic of the individual. If a test is valid from the 'construct' point of view, it can indicate the individual's actual achievement of instructional objectives. High construct validity for a test may be ensured by having quality individual test items and by tricking a proper balance between easy and difficult items.

Construct validity may be ascertained by the method of factorial analysis. This validity has special references to the areas of abilities and personality. Expect working in these areas have demonstrated that each of the above areas may be reduced to statistical elements called factors, for example: Thurston's factorial approach to mental abilities. A test which correlates with may one of the factors (e=verbal, numerical, spatial, reasoning, etc.) would be said to have factorial validity. Construct validity is used in such tests as those of study habit skills, appreciations, understandings and interpretation of data.

Face validity

Face validity means that the given test appears or seems to measure what it is to measure. This validity does not refer to what the test actually measure but refers to what the test seems to measure. After actual process, the test may or may not come out to be valid.

Predictive validity

Predictive validity determines the future success of test. We need a test having high predictive validity when we which to use it for predicting the future status of an individual. The predictive validity of a test is determined on the basis of an established criterion. For this purpose, the given test scores are correlated with data collected at a future date. For example, a new entrant to a class is given a new test of academic ability. At the end of the first term, grades on this test are correlated with each student's average grades for the term. In this case, these first-term grades are called the criterion. This criterion becomes the measure of validity.

Concurrent validity

Tests are said to have concurrent validity when they can distinguish between two or more groups of individuals whose status at the time of testing is different. For example, tests used to distinguish between persons with personality disorders and the Normal ones it successful, demonstrate concurrent validity. Such an example of a test is the Minnesota multiphase personality inventory.

PERSONAL DATA SHEET

To know the background of the Students, The investigator used personal data sheets along with the Developed Questionnaire. It asked for details of Gender, Students Locality, Types of School, Parent Occupation and School Locality. The students were asked to fill in all the particulars given in the personal data sheets.

SIZE OF THE SAMPLE

There are so many School's in Salem district among that the investigator select the 3 School's in random sampling method.

TABLE.13.3: List of Male and Female samples

S.No	Category	Students
1.	Male	72
2.	Female	78
Total		150

The present study is done by Normative Survey Method. The Stratified Random Sampling Technique was followed. The size of the Sampling was 150 Students only.

ADMINISTERING THE TOOL

The Opinonnairre were administered separately among the 150 Students,72 Male Students and 78 female Students of the following Sampling School's in Salem District. The name of the sampling Schools in Salem District following

TABLE.13.4: Name of the Sampling School's in Salem District from Which the Samples are Collected

S.No	Name of the Schools	District
1	Vedhha vikass Higher Secondary School	Salem District
2	Government Higher Secondary School	
3	Sri Saradha Ramakrishna Higher Secondary School	

The above table 13.4 shows the name and the district of the 3 School's from which the Samples are collected.

SCORING KEY

The Opinonnairre consists of 30 Positive Statements and 20 Negative Statements. The Negative questions were scored as 1/2/3/4 and positive questions were scored as 4/3/2/1. They are Strongly Agree, Agree, Disagree and Strongly Disagree. The total maximum scores for the Tools were 150 and the total minimum scores to the same are 50 respectively.

STATISTICAL TECHNIQUES

For the analysis of data following statistical technique were adopted. They were,

1. Arithmetic Mean
2. Standard Deviation
3. 't'–test

Arithmetic Mean

$$M = \frac{\sum fx}{N}$$

f = Frequency of each class interval

x = Mid point of each class

N = Total number of scores.

Standard Deviation

$$S = \sqrt{\frac{\sum fx^2}{N} - \frac{(\sum fx^2)}{N}} \times i$$

x = Deviation of each score from mean

N = Total number of score.

i = class interval

't' – test

$$t = \frac{m_1 - m_2}{\sqrt{\frac{SD_1^2}{N_1} - \frac{SD_1^2}{N_2}}}$$

m_1 = Mean of first sample

m_2 = Mean of second sample

SD_1 = Standard Deviation of first sample

SD_2 = Standard Deviation of second sample.

N_1 = Total Number of first sample

N_2 = Total Number of second sample

DELIMITATIONS OF THE STUDY

Broadly speaking, any study is impossible without limitation .Research studies is general will have delimitation due to many factors .This study too has some delimitations. It is the responsibility to the researches to see that the study is contacted with maximum care in ordered to be reliable

How ever, the following delimitations were unavoidable in the present study,

1. The study has been limited to Salem district only.
2. The study restricted to the higher secondary students only.
3. This study adopted survey method using Questionnaires to collect data from respondents.
4. A purposive stratified random sample was used to choose the subject to be included in the study.
5. This study is focused mainly on the variables, Gender, Students Locality, Types of School, Parent Occupation and School Locality.

❐

14

Analysis and Interpretation

Any research work could be meaningful when the data were analyzed and interpreted properly. Therefore the researcher has given much important to this part. The data collected from the sample analyzed and interpreted in the following heads.

a. Descriptive analysis
b. Differential analysis

DESCRIPTIVE ANALYSIS

It includes comparison of measures of central tendency such as the mean and the measures of variability such as standard deviation. The calculated values are used to describe the properties of the different sub-samples.

150 students from Salem District constituted the sample. The variable studied in the present judgment was with reference to some selected variables like. Gender, Types of School's, Locality of students, Locality of School's, Parents occupation.

After the data was collected, it was classified as the above mentioned variables

DIFFERENTIAL ANALYSIS

It contains the determinations of the statistical significance of the difference between references to selected variables. It contains 't' test. A 't' test is a numerical procedure that takes into account the difference between the means of the sample present in the scores. Thus the ' t' test is a technique to find out whether the difference the mean performance is significant or not.

LEVEL OF SIGNIFICANCE

Experimenters and research workers choose several arbitrary standards for their convenience. These arbitrary standards are called level of significance. Most commonly used level of significance is 0.01 and 0.05 level. For the present investigation, the researcher has used 0.05 levels as significance to analyze the existence of various hypotheses.

DIFFERENTIAL ANALYSIS

TABLE.14.1: Significant Differences between Aided boys and Aided Girls towards Awareness on Environmental Education among Higher Secondary Students

S. No.	Variables	N	Mean	Standard deviation	't' Value	Significant Level of 0. 05
1	Aided Boys	41	79.71	7.12	2.45*	1. 96
2	Aided Girls	34	83.44	5.99		

*-Significant **-No Significant

From the above table 14.1 .it shows calculated 't' value is less than the tabulated 't' value at 0.05 level of significance . We accept the null hypothesis .So there is no significant difference between Aided boys and Aided girls towards awareness on Environmental Education among Higher Secondary Students.

TABLE.14.2: Significant Differences between Boys and Girls towards Awareness on Environmental Education among Higher Secondary Students

S. No.	Variables	N	Mean	Standard deviation	't' Value	Significant Level of 0. 05
1	Boys	72	78.138	7.904	0.28**	1. 96
2	Girls	78	78.51	8.148		

*-Significant **-No Significant

From the above table 14.2 .It shows calculated 't' value is less than the tabulated 't' value at 0.05 level of significance . We accept the null hypothesis .So there is no significant different between boys and girls towards awareness on Environmental Education among Higher Secondary Students.

TABLE.14.3: Significant Difference between Rural and Urban Students towards Awareness on Environmental Education among Higher Secondary Students

S.No	Variables	N	Mean	Standard deviation	't' Value	Significant Level of 0. 05
1	Rural Students	79	78.25	10.96	0.29**	1. 97
2	Urban Students	71	78.7	7.884		

*-Significant **-No Significant

From the above table 14.3 .It shows calculated 't' value is less than the tabulated 't' value at 0.05 level of significance . We accept the null hypothesis .So there is no significant different between Rural and Urban Students towards awareness on Environmental Education among Higher Secondary Students.

TABLE.14.4: Significant Difference between Rural and Urban Schools towards Awareness on Environmental Education among Higher Secondary Students

S. No.	Variables	N	Mean	Standard deviation	't' Value	Significant Level of 0. 05
1	Rural Schools	75	75.4	7.972	4.86*	1. 97
2	Urban Schools	75	81.33	6.847		

*-Significant **-No Significant

From the above table 14.4 .It shows calculated 't' value is less than the tabulated 't' value at 0.05 level of significance . We Reject the null hypothesis .So there is no significant different between Rural and Urban Schools towards awareness on Environmental Education among Higher Secondary Students.

TABLE.14.5: Significant Difference between Government and Private Parent's Occupation towards Awareness on Environmental Education among Higher Secondary Students

S. No.	Variables	N	Mean	Standard deviation	't' Value	Significant Level of 0. 05
1	Government Parents Occupation	52	79.35	7.54	0.818*	1. 96
2	Private Parents Occupation	98	78.255	8.43		

*-Significant **-No Significant

From the above table 14.5 .It shows calculated 't' value is grater then the tabulated 't' value at 0.05 level of significance . We accepted the null hypothesis .So there is significant different between Government and Private Parent's Occupation towards awareness on Environmental Education among Higher Secondary Students.

TABLE.14.6: Significant Difference between Government Boys and Government Girls towards Awareness on Environmental Education among Higher Secondary Students

S. No.	Variables	N	Mean	Standard deviation	't' Value	Significant Level of 0. 05
1	Government Boys	31	76.39	6.36	1.19**	1. 96
2	Government Girls	44	74.48	7.43		

*-Significant **-No Significant

From the above table 14.5 .It shows calculated 't' value is grater then the tabulated 't' value at 0.05 level of significance. We accepted the null hypothesis. So there is significant different between Government Boys and Government Girls towards awareness on Environmental Education among Higher Secondary Students.

CONCLUSION

Thus the analysis of the data generated by the administration of the tool on the sample of 150 higher Secondary School Students at Salem District has yielded many interesting results. Which are summarized in the succeeding next chapter.

❐

15

Findings, Conclusions and Recommendations

In this chapter an attempt had been made to consolidate all the findings of the present study, the investigator also made some recommendation, which include the relevant area for this research and lastly the conclusion the findings are based on the result collected from the opinioned.

THE STUDY IN RESTROSPECT

The aim of the present investigation was to find out the "Awareness on Environmental Education among higher secondary students at Salem District".

METHODOLOGY IN BRIEF

For the present study normative survey method was adopted .for the sample of the study, 150 students of Salem District were collected .The tool used for the collection of data is Environmental Education awareness scale.

STATEMENT OF THE STUDY

The problem under the study is entitled as ***"Awareness on Environmental Education among Higher Secondary Students at Salem District".***

OBJECTIVES OF THE STUDY

The Major Objective of the study was to find out the level of Environmental Awareness. The Specific objectives are as follows.

MAIN OBJECTIVE

The first and foremost objective is to find out the Awareness on Environmental Education among Higher Secondary students at Salem District.

SPECIFIC OBJECTIVES

The specific objective is to find out the significant difference towards Awareness on Environmental Education among Higher secondary Students at Salem District is based on

1. Gender (Male/Female)
2. Student's Locality (Rural/Urban)
3. Types of school (Government/Aided)
4. Parent occupation (Government/Private)
5. School Locality (Rural/Urban)

The third Objectives are to find out the mean, Standard deviation on the various factors of the Awareness among Higher Secondary students.

MAJOR FINDINGS OF THE STUDY

From the present study the investigator came the following finding:

1. There is no significance difference between Aided boys and Aided girls towards awareness on Environmental education among Higher Secondary students.
2. There is no significance difference between Boys and Girls towards awareness on Environmental education among Higher Secondary students.
3. There is no significance difference between Rural and Urban students towards awareness on Environmental education among Higher Secondary students.
4. There is no significant different between Rural and Urban Schools towards awareness on Environmental education among Higher Secondary students.
5. There is significant different between Government and Private Parents Occupation towards awareness on Environmental education among Higher Secondary students.
6. There is significant different between Government Boys and Government Girls towards awareness on Environmental education among Higher Secondary students.

CONCLUSION OF THE STUDY

From the present study the investigator came to the following discussion and conclusion

1. Aided boys and Aided girls have a similar awareness on Environmental Education. Because Tamil Nadu Education System add Environment study in science subject.
2. Boys and Girls also have a similar awareness on Environmental Education. Because Tamil Nadu Education System add Environment study in science subject.
3. Urban Locality School students have more awareness on Environmental Education than Rural Locality School students. Because the Urban area students communicate with the surroundings and have gather more information about Environmental Education through many mass media.
4. Parental occupation of government parents and private school parents also have the similar awareness on Environmental Education. Because awareness on Environmental Education is not based on parental occupation.
5. Urban school students and rural school have similar awareness on Environmental Education. Because the teachers asked their students to planning the plant is the school surroundings and develops the knowledge of importance of Environment in their life.
6. Government Boys and Government Girls also have a similar awareness on Environmental Education .Because Tamil Nadu Education System add Environment study in science subject.

SUGGESTIONS FOR ENVIRONMENTAL STUDIES

1. The present study is limited to students studying in classes XI-XII. Similar studies can be conducted for students after secondary and senior secondary stage.
2. A similar study can be conducted to compare the environmental awareness of rural and urban students.
3. Present study has been conducted by using only three models of teaching. Similar studies can be undertaken by using many other models of teaching.
4. The present study confined only to the students. Similar studies can be extended to compare environmental awareness of teachers of different schools.

5. Studies can be conducted to find out the effectiveness of various models of teaching in different subjects in different schools and across different districts.

EDUCATION IMPLICATIONS OF THE STUDY

1. More measures are to the taken at rural and urban schools to create Environmental Education awareness.
2. More programmers related to Environmental Education awareness are to be conducted to the students.
3. The students may be trained to give some activist like quiz debit discussion, seminar, workshop etc., on Environmental Education awareness.
4. The teacher may be trained to teach their lesson linked with Environmental Education.
5. Government Should introduce and enrich awareness on Environmental Education programmers
6. The government has to modify the syllabus according the needs and mental level of students.

AREAS OF RESEARCH FOR THE FUTURE

Research is a chain activity. There purpose of any research in education is to find solutions for problems related to teachers, students, learning etc… But one problem always leaves many related research questions that can be investigated by other researchers, some of the areas for research in the future may be as follows,

1. The present study can be repeated with wide sample.
2. A similar study can be conducted on the professional school students.
3. A Study can be conducted to find out the demographic and motivational variable associated with Environmental Education activities.
4. A similar study can be conducted on the higher secondary school students.
5. The present study could be undertaken at various states in India.
6. A study can be conducted on the primary, secondary and Higher Secondary school teachers.
7. The gender difference in Environmental Education awareness can be studied.
8. Development of CA, package on the awareness on Environmental Education.
9. A study on the modern techniques to develop the awareness on Environmental Education among the D.T.Ed training students.
10. A comparative study on the awareness on Environmental Education

among the students of different categories like secondary and higher secondary students.

11. A critical on evolving strategies promoting the awareness on Environmental Education among the arts and science students.

CONCLUSION

The present study made on awareness on Environmental Education among Higher Secondary students. The findings of the present study revel that the Higher Secondary students having awareness among Gender, Type of college, marital status, Locality, Challenged persons from the samples families, with respect to the questionnaire.

❐

Bibliography

1. Clifford T. Morgan, Richard A king, John R Weirz, John Schopler, Introduction Psychology Pp.645-630
2. Denis. M, E. Mellet and S. Kosslyn(2004), Neuroimaging of Mental Imagery, Psychology Press, An introduction, European Journal of Cognitive Psychology, Pp.625 - 630
3. Elhaney Sandra. MC (1993) Children's mental health and their ability to learn,Journal of National health and education Consortium, Pp.22 - 50
4. Felix, Robert H. (1957), "Evolution of community concepts," Medical Journal of Psychiatry P. P 183 - 195
5. Haught Manson J.W. (1975) A historical view of stress field" Journal of human stress. Pp.130 - 165
6. Jahada (1963) " Mental Health – Book" Vol-3, Pp.1067-1079
7. Lacan. J (1985)., Sign, Symbol and Imagery in M. Blonsky (Ed). On Signs, Blackwell, Oxford Pp.238 - 247
8. Richard. D (2012). Coping with stress predicts school grades, life safe satisfaction and feeling about high school, learning and individual difference, Vol.22/2,Pp.235-241
9. Leung (2010). A protective factor buffer against the academic stress of school –aged children, Educational psychology, Vol.30/4,Pp.395 -410
10. David. C (2009). Chinese international students academic stress in the united status. College students journal, Vol.143/4, Pp.939 – 960
11. Bartone, Paul. T (2009). Academic stress and health, Exploring the moderating Role of personality Hardiness, Scandinavian journal of educational research, Vol.53/5,Pp.421-429

12. Daniel. F.K (2010). Academic stress and anxiety in children, the role of paternal support, Journal of child and family studies, Vol.19/I,Pp.90 -100
13. Paige. D (2009). School Related stress and depression in Adolescents with and without Learning Disabilities, An Exploratory study, Alberta of educational research, Vol.55/1,Pp.92 -108
14. Laura. J.(2012). Stress and anxiety surrounding forth coming standard assessment tests in english school children, pastoral care in education, Vol.33/4, Pp.289-302.
15. Adrian Furnham and Petrides K.V (2003).Trait Emotional Intelligence and Happiness, *Social Behavior and Personality*, 31(8), pp.815-824.
16. Angner.E.(2011). The evolution of empathic: *The historical roots of subjective measures of well being. International Journal of Wellbeing,* 1(1), 4 - 41.
17. Anastasi, A.(1961). Psychological Testing (2ndedition). New York: The Macmillan Company.
18. Calgary Alberta June (2012).Compiled by William Tillier, Positive psychology.
19. Chris Barker and Brian Martiny (2011). Participation: The Happiness Connection. *Journal of Public Deliberation,* Volume 7, Issue 1 , Article 9.
20. Deepti Hooda (Jan 2009).Social Intelligence as a Predictor of Positive Psychological Health, *Journal of the Indian Academy of Applied Psychology,* Vol. 35, No.1, pp.143-150.
21. Dr. Debleena Kumar (2013).The relation of stressful life events and a happy life. *International Journal of Social Science & Interdisciplinary Research,2* (2)
22. Howard Gardner (1983). Frames of Mind, P.243.
23. Katy W.Y. Liu (2012). Humor Styles, Self-Esteem and Subjective Happiness, *Discovery – SS Student E-Journal,* Vol. 1, pp.21-41.
24. Rik Linssen, Luuk van Kempen and Gerbert Kraaykamp (2011). Subjective Well-being in Rural India: The Curse of Conspicuous Consumption, *Soc Indic Res,* 101, pp.57–72.
25. Ruchi Thakur, Shubhangana Sharma and Raj Pathania (2013). Social Intelligence of Adolescents: A Study of Himachal Pradesh, *Stud Home Com Sci,* 7(3), pp.161-166.
26. Seyed Mohammad Kalantarkousheh, Naeimeh Nickamal, Zahra Amanollahi, and Elahe Dehghani (2014).Spiritual Intelligence and life satisfaction among married and unmarried females, *Open Journal of Social Sciences,* 2,pp.172-177.

27. Sreekumar, R (April 2008). The Pattern of Association of Religious Factors with Subjective Well-Being: A Path Analysis Model, *Journal of the Indian Academy of Applied Psychology,* Vol. 34, pp.119-125.
28. Tayfun Dogan and Ali Eryilmaz (2013).The Role of Social Intelligence in Happiness, *Creation Journal of Education,* 16, pp.863-878.
29. Aditi Sharma. (2005) – "Environmental studies", New Delhi:Surjeet Publications.
30. Agarwal, V.K and Usha Guota. (2002) "Ecology and Ethiology",New Delhi:S.Chand and Co.
31. Amandeep Karu,etal.(2006)-"Scientific approach to Environmental Education", Ludihiana:Tandon Publications.
32. Ananthakrishnan,.T.N. (1987) - "Bio-resources Ecology", New Delhi:Oxford IBH Publishing Company Pvt Ltd.
33. Bogerrider.A.and Klein.R. (1982) - "Does Solar UV influence the competitive relationship in higher plants", Newyork.
34 Brown.Sandra, Iverson, L.R., Anantha Prasad and Logo, A.E.(1993) – Estimating Biomass and Biomass Change of Tropical Forests, CAIAC Communications.18:7.
35. Boyce Ann. (1997) - "Introduction to Environmental technology", New York:van Nostrand Reinhold International Thomson Pub.Inc.
36. Chandra Pal, "Environmental Pollution and Development", Delhi:Mittal Publications.
37. Despande,S.D. (1983) - Modelling of the Atmospheric Minor constituents. Proc. Work-ship on Global Ozone Problem.National Physical lab., New Delhi:pp.14-52.
38. Eugence P.Odum.(1996)-"Fundamental of Ecology 3rdEdn)", Dehradun: Nataraj Publications,
39. Fox, F.M., and Caldwell, M.M. (1978) - Competitive interaction in plants populations exposed to supplementary UV-B radiations. Oecologia (Berl) 36:pp.137-90
40. Ghai, Dharam (1995) – Global Markets, Global Insecurity. Our planet, 7(3): pp.6-8.
41. Ghanta, R.anmd rao.D.B. (2001) - "Environmental Education, Problems and Prospects", New Delhi: Australia:Blackwell Publishing Company.
42 Kumar, V.K. (1982) - "A study in Environmental pollution", Varanasi:Tara Book nagency.
43. Mookerjee, Anjali.(1983)-Ultraviolet Effect on Unicellular organisms in presence of drugs. proc.Indo-US Workshop on Global Ozone problem.Nat.Physical Lab.,New Delhi:pp.227-30.

44. Maduraj - "Emerging Trend in Environmental pollution", Delhi :IVY Publications, 2001.
45. Radha, S.and Sankhyan, A.S. "Environmental Challenges of the 21st century", New Delhi:Deep and DEEp publications.
46. Saxena, A.B. (1986) - "Environmental Education", Agra: National Psychological corporation
47. Sharma, B.K. - "Ecology and Environment", Meerut:Rastogi Publications.
48. Singh, S.and Dubey. (1989) - "A Environmental Management", Allahabad:Dept of geography, Allahabad university.
49. Singh, S.(1995). "Environmental Geography", Allahabad:Prayog Pustak bhawan.
50. Shukla R.s and Chandel, P.S. (1992) - "Plant Ecology", New Delhi:S. Chand and Co.,.
51. Shukla.S.K and Srivatava P.R "Evaluation of Environmental Noise Pollution", New Dlhi: commonwealth Publications.
52. Susils Appadurai. (2004) - "Environmental Studies", Chennai: New Century Book House.
53. Thangamani and Shymala Thangamani,"A Text Book of Environmental Studies", Sivakasi:Pranav Syndicate publications.
54. Trivedi R.N. (1997)-"A Text book of Environmental Sciences",New Delhi: Anmol Publications Pvt.Ltd.
55. Verma, P.S and Agarwal.,"K.Environmental Biology" (Principles of Ecology), New Delhi:S.Chand and Company.
56. Williams,T.Mooon.A and Willians.m.(1991)-"Environment and Helath",Delhi: B.R.Publishing Corporation.

❑❑❑